ONE LORD, ONE CHURCH

WORLD
CHRISTIAN
BOOKS

ONE LORD,
ONE CHURCH

by J. ROBERT NELSON

ASSOCIATION PRESS, NEW YORK

ONE LORD, ONE CHURCH

Copyright © 1958 by
J. Robert Nelson

Association Press, 291 Broadway, New York 7, N. Y.

The series *World Christian Books* is sponsored by the International Missionary Council in co-operation with the Christian Literature Council of Great Britain and the Committee on World Literacy and Christian Literature of the United States. This volume, under the same title, is published in Great Britain by the United Society for Christian Literature (Lutterworth Press, London), 1958. The Scripture quotations in this book are from the Revised Standard Version of the Bible.

Price, $1.25

Library of Congress catalog card number: 58-11535

55

Printed in the United States of America
American Book–Stratford Press, Inc., New York

ABOUT WORLD CHRISTIAN BOOKS

TODAY it is not enough to believe; it is necessary also to understand. From every part of the world comes the demand for books that will help the Christian to understand his faith, to find the answers to the questions that he and other men are asking, and to know how to present the faith to others. The series WORLD CHRISTIAN BOOKS is planned to help in this particular area of Christian need. The books are directed in the first place to the "younger churches," but the old distinction between younger and older churches no longer really holds. All churches are faced by the same problems. In all countries the same questions are being asked. The series is specially planned for those who are called to preach and teach, in the hope that the materials given in these books may help them to carry out their task more effectively. But the aim has also been to write so simply that ordinary members of the church who wish to study their faith may be able to use these books as individuals or in study groups and so to grow in knowledge and understanding.

The books are being published first in English, but it is intended that as soon as possible they should be made available in the main languages of the Christian world. Writers have been chosen from various countries and various branches of the church, with special emphasis on the younger churches. This means that there will be a variety of voices, but the aim and the hope is that through many minds and many tongues the faith of the church in its one Lord may be clearly set forth.

STEPHEN NEILL
General Editor

Contents

Contents

chapter **1**

Jesus Christ Has Made
Us One

WHY IS THERE so much concern today about Christian unity? If the problem of unity could be ignored, life would be much easier for most Christians in most places. The fact that differences of doctrine prevent all members of the family of Christ from receiving his Supper at the same table would then cause no anguish of spirit. The open competition of Christian churches, preaching the same gospel from the same Bible in the same village, to the confusion of the same non-Christian people, would be no scandal. Each little band of Christians could feel complacent and contented in its isolation from neighboring churches. Each denomination could pursue its own program of evangelism and social service without thinking of the others. All this could be true except for one thing: *that Jesus Christ wills his Church to be one in mind, spirit, life, and witness.*

The teaching of the Bible about the essential oneness of the Church is perfectly clear. It does not give us a detailed plan for the form or structure of unity. But it leaves no doubt that the work of Jesus Christ was "to gather into one the children of God who are scattered abroad" (John 11:52), and to reconcile all who believe in one community of love.

Christians are not the only ones who speak of their unity. More and more the word is used in the sphere of politics—of the United Nations, of the various blocs of nations, or states, tribes, and regions within the same nation. Trade unions speak of their unity. So do Communists. So do the hundreds of fraternal clubs, societies, orders, and lodges. Moreover, there are definite appeals to the unity of the adherents of various religions: Buddhists, Shintoists, Hindus, Muslims. And many people today speak with increasing fervor of the need for a unity of all religions of the world. Unity is a popular and universal word today; but people are disunited as to its proper meaning and application.

Christians preserve a distinct and unique meaning of unity. It applies to their common relation to God in Jesus Christ and their mutual relations to one another. Therefore it is essentially a word about the Church. Christians may well be eager to promote unity among persons, groups, and nations for the order and peace of human society. When they work for this broader unity of mankind, however, they are striving for an ideal which thus far in history has relatively little reality. Today it is so easy for many people to travel about the world that persons having the same loyalties and problems naturally want to get together. Yet there is something arbitrary and artificial about even the most worthy efforts to achieve closer unity among people who have relatively little in common.

Christians of the world, on the contrary, have very

much in common. What they have is not just a common history or language or geographical boundary. Such things are temporary and passing, earth-bound and finite. Christian unity is based upon that which is eternal and divine, namely, the choosing and calling of his people by Almighty God, the incarnation of the eternal Word of God in the person of Jesus Christ, his death and resurrection, and the giving of the Holy Spirit. If Christians were united only by their memory of a single religious teacher and loyalty to the Bible, their unity would be real but very frail. But Christian unity consists of common participation in the special and decisive gift of God himself. "There is one body and one Spirit . . . one hope . . . one Lord, one faith, one baptism, one God and Father of us all" (Eph. 4:4–6).

When a Christian from an Indian village meets a Christian from a European farm or a Japanese city, differences in language, culture, and color are of no essential importance. What counts is the bare and primal fact that he, like them, believes in the one God and Father of Jesus Christ, that he confesses the same gospel of salvation, and shares in the same baptism of water and the Holy Spirit. This makes the Indian, the European, and the Japanese to be brothers in a sense even deeper than their blood-related brotherhood in the family. "Here are my mother and my brothers!" said Jesus. "Whoever does the will of God is my brother, and sister, and mother" (Mark 3:34–35).

The New Testament has many ways of referring to the Church and its unity. It speaks in parables and images rather than with the prosaic directness of a book of history or science. Most of us, when asked to define the Church and its unity, would describe the organization of

11

a congregation or of a denomination, and would tell of their interrelationships and the kind of work and witness carried on by these Christians in the world. But the New Testament has very little of such description. It is concerned more with the nature and quality of the Church's relation to Jesus Christ and of the mutual relationships of Christians as persons. For this purpose it makes free and imaginative use of many figures of speech.

Christian unity is first of all the unity of the Church *with* Christ. Christians know Jesus Christ not as a long-buried hero, but as risen and living Lord. This faith in the continued presence of the Lord is attested in worship, witness, and life in the Christian community. The continuance of the Church through so many centuries, with its frequent movements of renewal and power, is a consequence of the Lord's promise, "And lo, I am with you always, to the close of the age" (Matt. 28:20).

The writers of the Gospels, as well as the Apostle Paul, attach much importance to the bond of unity between Christ and the Church. The Fourth Gospel presents Jesus as the one Shepherd of the faithful flock of sheep. This is a metaphor which is used frequently in the Old Testament as well as in the New. Raising sheep is still a major occupation of the land once called Palestine. Early readers could readily understand the power of the shepherd over his flock, as well as his responsibility for its safety and welfare. God himself was thought of as Shepherd in Psalm 23, and again in 95:7, "For he is our God, and we are the people of his pasture, and the sheep of his hand." But in Ezekiel 34:23, it is King David whom God appoints as shepherd over his people. And in the Gospels this role has devolved upon Jesus. As the Son of God and Messiah, Jesus gave this title a distinctive and abiding meaning, for he sought out and found the "lost sheep of the house of Israel" (Matt. 10:6; 15:24; 18:11–14), and he laid down his life for the sheep (John 10:15). Jesus is thus the sovereign Lord of the Church as well as the suffering Servant. And the intimacy of the relation between Christ and the Church is shown in the deeply personal bond between him and the faithful disciples. "I know my own and my own know me, as the Father knows me and I know the Father" (John 10:14–15). This comparison of the bond between the Father and the Son with that existing between the Son and his followers reminds us of the classic verse concerning unity (John 17:21), where the oneness of Christians is likened to that of God the Father and his Son.

In human experience the most intimate relationship known is that existing between husband and wife. To be sure, there are exceptions. Sometimes married partners are isolated from one another by suspicion, jealousy, or actual dislike. The relations of family members or just of good friends can be exceedingly close. Nevertheless, the human bond which normally is most intimate is that of marriage. The biblical teaching holds that man and woman grow into such perfect unity in love that they can almost be regarded as one person. Accepting this view of the marital union, the writer of the Letter to the Ephesians declares that Jesus Christ is the bridegroom and the Church his bride, whom he loved and for whose sake he gave himself up (Eph. 5:23–27). Indeed, the union between Christ and the Church is so close that it is *this* union which must be understood as the pattern and ideal for human marriage.

Another suggestive metaphor employed by John is that of the vine and the branches (15:1–8). At first this seems

13

rather impersonal. Yet its appropriateness and meaning are unmistakable. Once again Jesus chose as an image of himself something known to everyone in a vine-growing country. The whole vine includes all its branches. Yet a branch has its own identity; it lives from the source of life within the vine; it makes its contribution to the whole vine, and if it is healthy it bears grapes; but if it is fruitless (see Matt. 7:16–20) it is cut off and burned. The essential words in John 15 are these: "Abide in me, and I in you" (vs. 4). Here are the exhortation and promise which point to the unending unity between Jesus Christ and his Church.

The Apostle Paul emphasizes this relationship in his numerous repetitions of the phrase "in Christ," "with Christ," and "Christ in me." Paul declares, "If any one is in Christ, he is a new creation" (2 Cor. 5:17). Teaching the deepest meaning of baptism, he writes, "If we have been united with him in a death like his, we shall certainly be united with him in a resurrection like his" (Rom. 6:5). And in a joyous testimony to the reality of his faith Paul seems to shout through the printed words, "It is no longer I who live, but Christ who lives in me" (Gal. 2:20). Certainly Paul was a man who experienced the truth of Jesus' words of promise, "Abide in me, and I in you."

Paul's words about this close personal relation of Jesus Christ are unlike those of a non-Christian mystic. To be "in Christ" does not mean having an exalted, emotional experience of Christ's presence. Neither did Paul write about the single believer's sense of mystical identity with Christ. Always foremost in Paul's teaching was the whole Christian community, the Church. And the Christian simply cannot separate his faith in Jesus Christ from his membership in the whole Christian fellowship. A Christian is inevitably a member of Christ's people. So that, according to Paul's teaching rightly understood, a person who is "in Christ" is one who is "in the Church."

This understanding of "in Christ" has much importance for our grasp of the meaning of the Church's unity with Christ. It may be said of the Church as a whole, as Paul said of himself: "It is no longer I who live, but Christ who lives in me." This oneness between the Lord and his people is essential to the life and nature of the Church. It is true of the Church in every variety of its earthly form. Whether the congregation worships in the simplicity of a mud-brick chapel with thatched roof, or in the splendor of a great stone cathedral, it is the Church only in so far as it is one with Christ. When Ignatius of Antioch, a second-century martyr, wrote his famous words, "Where Jesus Christ is, there is the catholic Church," he was simply interpreting the promise made by Jesus himself, "Where two or three are gathered in my name, there am I in the midst of them" (Matt. 18:20).

While Christian unity is primarily a oneness between the living Lord and the whole Church, it is also a unity of faithful persons with one another. This is only another way of expressing the two great commandments taught by Jesus, to love the Lord God with all your heart and to love your neighbor as yourself. Against these commandments one can hardly protest. Most people, whether Christian or not, are ready to accept them as ideal precepts for life. But, as everyone knows in his own experience, it is much easier to accept a precept than to live by it. The Apostle Paul expressed the universal sense of frustration and defeat when he cried, "I can will what is right, but I cannot do it" (Rom. 7:18). Lest he appear to despair of fulfilling the law of God, however, he elsewhere exults, "But thanks be to God, who in Christ always leads us in triumph" (2 Cor. 2:14), "for the love of Christ controls us" (2 Cor. 5:14).

Paul was convinced that there was a divine power at work within the Christian fellowship, and within him personally as a member of it. This power preserves faithful men and women from yielding to evil in despair, and enables them to live together in love. Even though the members are weak and sinful still, so that strife arises within the local churches, Christ abides as the living Spirit of love within the community. Without the presence of Jesus Christ as the one who both teaches the will of God and enables people to obey it, the Christian's moral life is hopeless. Without this presence of him who commanded the disciples, that nucleus of the early Church, "Love one another as I have loved you" (John 15:12), the inner unity of the Church is impossible.

Various images are used by the New Testament to express this inner unity. They describe not an ideal state of peace and harmony after which Christians are urged to strive. Instead they convey the good news that God in Jesus Christ has actually done something to empower them to enjoy this unity.

The symbol of division is a wall. The wall which seemingly could be neither surmounted nor destroyed was that which separated Jews from Gentiles (or simply non-Jews). The attitude of the ancient orthodox Jew to persons of other nations or religions was as strictly exclusive as that of a Hindu Brahman to a sweeper of the lowest caste. There was actually a wall about the courtyard of the Temple in Jerusalem, which prevented all non-Jews from gaining access to the holy place. The stones of this wall

16

of separation were like the numerous religious laws affecting personal purity and ritual perfection. To the Jewish mind these laws were placed securely like stones and sealed with mortar by God himself. It was his will, they believed, that there should be absolutely no contact with the unclean foreigner.

But what was the Christian message to the despised and rejected Gentiles? These astonishing words: "Remember that you were . . . alienated from the commonwealth of Israel. . . . But now in Christ Jesus you who once were far off have been brought near in the blood of Christ. For he is our peace, who has made us both one, and has broken down the dividing wall of hostility" (Eph. 2:12–14). And what was spoken to the exclusive Jew? That Christ has accomplished this reconciling work "by abolishing in his flesh the law of commandments and ordinances, that he might create in himself one new man in place of the two, so making peace, and might reconcile us both to God in one body through the cross" (vss. 15–16).

In other words, the testimony of God's love in the humiliation and death of his Son Jesus Christ was so powerful that it cracked open even that formidable barrier to human fellowship. Henceforth the chosen people of God was not confined to the Jewish nation, but extended to all men and women everywhere who accept the gospel and confess Jesus Christ as Lord. In Christ's death the barriers of cult, class, and race were brought to an end. There is place in the Christian community for all persons who have faith. As Paul declared, "There is neither Jew nor Greek, there is neither slave nor free, there is neither male nor female; for you are all one in Christ Jesus" (Gal. 3:28).

The New Testament often says that the Church, in which this wonderful quality of personal unity is found, is the "body of Christ." What does this mean? One needs little imagination to understand the meaning of the body as a physical organism in which every single organ or part is dependent upon other parts as well as upon the life of the whole body. The mutual dependence of eye and ear, hand and foot, is the model of the common aid and support which individual Christians should give to one another. "If one member suffers, all suffer together; if one member is honored, all rejoice together" (1 Cor. 12:26). This kind of picture can be applied very simply to the personal relationships within the Christian fellowship. A healthy church, like a healthy body, is one in which there is no discord.

We miss the strength of Paul's teaching, however, if we see in 1 Corinthians 12 a mere object lesson which could be applied just as well to any human society as to the Church. Paul emphasizes what God has done by his Spirit to make possible this desired unity. By the one Spirit, God has given varieties of gifts or talents to individual members of the Church. Knowing the diverse needs and temperaments of his creatures, God has given to each one a certain ability which is useful for the well-being of the whole community. Some are able to heal, some to prophesy, some to speak wisdom, others to teach, to manage domestic affairs. These differences of gifts of the Spirit are not excuses for dissension or division in the Church. Just the contrary. They are intended by God to hold the members together in unity, since each needs the other. And the crowning gift of all, which is available to all members and not just to a few, is the very love of God,

18

"which binds everything together in perfect harmony" (Col. 3:14; see 1 Cor. 13).

All this teaching may seem very theoretical to those who have seen too much dissension and bitterness within the church to be impressed by pious thoughts about unity. It was easy enough for Paul to write such ideas—but he should just see the contentious people in *my* church!

If there was anyone who had cause to despair of the peace and concord of the Christian community, it was the Apostle Paul. Read all that he wrote to the young church at Corinth. What fearful sins they committed! Jealousy, strife, arrogance, incest, bitter lawsuits, idolatry, prostitution, drunkenness, gluttony—all these are cited by the Apostle as sins of the Corinthians. We might well ask if any congregation has been so guilty of unchristian living. And yet, to these same people Paul writes, "Now you are the body of Christ" (12:27). He was surely no optimistic theorist. He knew the dark and shameful side of church life. But even more, he knew the reality of God's grace given to men in Jesus Christ, and he received in faith the revelation of God's will for the unity of his people.

So also the first converts in Jerusalem and Antioch learned about Christian unity, not by theoretical discussion but by living together. They learned first of all the truth that Jesus Christ had broken down the dividing wall of hostility. Natural and cultural differences among Christians simply could not prevent the unitive power of Christ from holding them together in fellowship. When severe tension arose between those who insisted on retaining the Jewish sign of circumcision and those who said this was intolerable for Gentiles, there was a danger that the Church might divide permanently into parties or "denominations."

19

But Peter, James, and Paul did not allow this to happen.

Why this strange new solidarity? Did it depend only upon their common loyalty to their Lord Jesus? The cohesive power of such faith was indeed strong. But a still stronger power was that which arose not alone from men's wills but from the presence of God as Holy Spirit. The members of the early Church "devoted themselves to . . . fellowship" (Acts 2:42). Our weak word "fellowship" is used to translate the strong and rich Greek word *koinonia*. From the New Testament as a whole we learn that this word, which aptly describes the quality of the Church's life, has a number of meanings. It refers to the common ownership of property as well as the sharing of goods, as in an interchurch aid collection for the poor Christians of Jerusalem. It means the common profit from and sharing in the gifts of the Holy Spirit. Or it describes the Christians' participation in the divine life of the Spirit himself. Finally it means the common personal sharing in the body and blood of Jesus Christ in the sacrament of Holy Communion, when bread and wine become the means of divine grace.

In those early years of the Church the fellowship of Christians was threatened by inner tensions, and by the temptation to cling to non-Christian ways. Yet these members of the New Testament Church testified to the experienced reality of the amazing *koinonia*-life in the presence and power of the Holy Spirit. When dissension among the brethren seemed to threaten this corporate life, the Apostle Paul could confidently beg them "to maintain the unity of the Spirit in the bond of peace" (Eph. 4:3).

Moreover, he could assure them that the body of Christ in which they shared their common life was granted its unity for a special purpose in the mind of God. Even as

Christ came into the world and identified himself with human beings in order to reconcile them to God, so also he came "to unite all things in him, things in heaven and things on earth" (Eph. 1:10). This was his concise way of writing about the ultimate purpose of God, "the mystery of his will." Against all the evil force in the world, which causes rebellion against God and vicious strife among men, the Creator of the world contends. God's momentous and decisive attack against the divisive powers of evil was the sending of Jesus Christ. The unity of the Church is one of the early fruits of Christ's victory. This unity is a primary part of God's plan. It is a necessary mark of the Church which God has sent forth into the world to proclaim and extend the reconciling work of Christ. The Church's unity, therefore, is both a sign of that perfect unity which is to come in the kingdom of God and a means by which God will bring it to consummation. The Church must be one if it is to be used by God for unifying all the world in Christ.

chapter **2**

Healthy Diversity and Unhappy Divisions

U NTIL ONE UNDERSTANDS the biblical teaching about the unity of the Church with Christ and in Christ, he cannot be deeply disturbed over divisions in the Church. But once he sees how essential the Church is to the great reconciling work of God in Jesus Christ, he will know the pain and horror of these divisions. The trouble is that we can grow so accustomed to evils that we are no longer sensitive to them. In lands of poverty and famine a person may lose much compassion for the destitute and hungry and, contrary to his own conscience, simply accept them as part of the scene. Soldiers who at home would show sympathy for a man slightly crippled become callous in the heat of battle to the savagery and killing. And most Christians, for whose unity Jesus Christ was willing to die, are unmoved by the spectacle of party strife within congregations, of churches separated by racial differences, or of the proximity on the same street of churches of opposed denominations. For these it would be almost meaningless to offer the familiar prayer, ". . . give us grace

22

seriously to lay to heart the great dangers we are in by our unhappy divisions. . . ." But the divisions of the churches are dangerous and abhorrent to those who know and live by the New Testament faith.

A man may be justly puzzled, however, as to how far the New Testament is relevant to the churches of the present time. After all, these many centuries of history have brought great changes. Can the same principle of unity which applied to the tiny scattered congregations of the Roman Empire be considered valid for our own present earth-girding structure of churches? Consider one main question, for example. When the early Christians spoke of unity and division, they referred to the relations between individuals or small groups within the same church. But today we have to consider great and distinct families of churches, called confessions or communions, such as the Orthodox, Roman, Anglican, Lutheran, Reformed, Methodist, Baptist, Congregational, Pentecostal, etc. What a confusing array this would have been to the apostles! And in many countries the churches of these families are organized into separate denominations, the like of which was neither known nor anticipated by the New Testament.

It is perfectly clear that according to the Bible the Church exists on two levels only. There is the one Church Universal on earth and in heaven. And there is the local congregation which is the focal point of the Church. In between there are no communions or denominations, as we know them now. So it is simply not in accordance with the New Testament when we call these bodies the Lutheran Church, the Methodist Church, or the Roman Catholic Church. Yet it is precisely the separation of these bodies, whether in villages, cities, nations, or the world, which constitutes the problem of division. So, once again, what is the relevance of the New Testament teaching?

The New Testament has a very definite word for denominations. It addresses them negatively and in judgment. It calls into question their right to exist as separate and divided bodies.

First, we are certainly in error if we try to justify our denominations by any appeal to the Holy Scriptures. It is wrong for any denomination or communion to say that it alone is the bride of Christ or the body of Christ. An Anglican bishop recently quoted the words: "Christ loved the church and gave himself up for her" (Eph. 5:25) and then observed: "Christ did not love the Anglicans, or Orthodox or Baptists; he loved the Church." So it follows that no denomination can baptize a person into itself, but only into the one Church of Christ. And baptism is thus one of the strongest bonds of unity among all Christians.

Sometimes Christians misinterpret the Bible, when they apply to their denominations what the Bible says about individual believers. Consider, for example, the parable of the vine and the branches (John 15). Jesus is clearly speaking of his disciples as the branches. But some persons wrongly think of the various denominations as necessary branches of the one Church. Likewise, when Jesus prays "that they may all be one" (John 17:21), he is pleading with God for the unity of his followers. The word "they" does not refer to denominations which he wants to be merged. A similar temptation is presented by Paul's discourse on the diversities of the gifts of the Spirit (1 Cor. 12). Some Christians say that the different denominations are necessary because they embody the diversities of spiritual gifts which are given by God for the

24

wholeness of the Church. But this again is an arbitrary and illicit way of using the Bible to defend a nonbiblical idea.

In the second place, the New Testament implies that denominationalism is contrary to the true nature of the unity of the Church. The groups most nearly like denominations in the time of the apostles, so far as we know, were the three parties in Corinth which said they belonged to Paul, Apollos, or Cephas (1 Cor. 1:12). To compare these small groups to the large, well-organized, self-sufficient denominations of our present time is hardly fair. Nevertheless, the attack of the Apostle upon such a spirit of division in the early Church can be directed with equal justification toward present denominationalism. "Is Christ divided?" There is the critical question. For if Christ were somehow divided, the Church would be too. But Christ is one and indivisible, and so must the Church be. What is the source of such division? Paul answers: it is the carnal, sinful disposition of Christians, who forget they are living "in Christ" and act instead like "ordinary men" (1 Cor. 3:3-4).

When a sincere Christian begins to ponder the matter of divisions, his first conclusion may be that it is better for the Church to suffer divisions than to be exactly uniform everywhere. In many areas of the world today we have seen the growth of the totalitarian state and society. The dictator-state could not function without the unchallenged power of making men conform to its wishes. And most of those who are made to conform learn for the first time how precious is the privilege of liberty.

Now there is a widespread fear among Christians that the unity of the Church must depend upon the suppression of liberty and the imposition of a rigidly uniform pattern of doctrine, worship, government, and moral discipline. Those who are subject to such fear see only two alternatives for the Church: division or uniformity. Two things can be said, with a view to dispelling this fear. First, there is no church or denomination, not even the Roman Catholic, which at the present time imposes complete uniformity upon its own people. Variations of worship and religious thought are common in the Roman Catholic Church. Furthermore, no responsible church leader who advocates unity regards complete uniformity as anything but an evil to be avoided. This has been emphasized repeatedly by nearly all such leaders.

Secondly, a clear distinction must be made between the words "diversity" or "difference" on the one hand and "division" on the other. That there are divisions among the churches is a fact to be deplored. That there are diversities and differences among the churches is a sign of their health and strength. Yet people often make the mistake of deploring the "differences" between the churches, as though these were the same as "divisions."

We welcome diversities or differences just because God made all men to be individuals and not like coins stamped by the same machine. Some of us were born in hot climates, some in cold. We were born as members of many different races and nations, and from childhood we learned one of the hundreds of distinct languages. Some of us are strictly controlled by orderliness, reasonableness, and punctuality, while others are inherently casual and emotional, guided more by feeling than by reasoning. Our tastes in music and art are different; our systems of education and hence our ways of thinking are different; our views as to what actions are polite or rude differ according to cultures. In short, the very diversity of mankind

26

makes it inevitable that so great a body as the Church must and should reflect these diversities in numerous ways. And the Christian faith is so comprehensive and universally valid that it can embrace all these God-given diversities without alienating a person from his own country or straining the unity of the Church.

What about liberty of thought and belief? Would not a church which is fully united be so bound to a credal and doctrinal system that it would stifle any deviations of thought in teaching and preaching? This is a question which seriously disturbs many of us when we think about unity. But how well founded is the fear? There are some indeed who oppose the movement toward church unity for precisely the opposite reason. They expect the patterns of belief in a united church to be so vaguely and carelessly defined that any kind of false teaching may be tolerated. The former is the fear of those who set too high a value on complete freedom of thought in the Church. The latter is the fear of those who do not appreciate its value. Those at one extreme would gladly abolish all creeds and confessions as man-made devices for enslaving men's minds. Those at the opposite extreme regard their creeds and confessions as being virtually of divine authority.

Is there a way between these? Yes, it is the way of a quite legitimate diversity within unity of belief. And this diversity is already there to a far greater extent than most people realize. Within those church families which do not require adherence to any formal creed or statement of faith there is nevertheless a high degree of consensus on those essentials of faith without which Christianity loses its distinctive character. These essentials include belief in God as Father, Son, and Holy Spirit; salvation through

27

the death and resurrection of Jesus Christ; the authority and sufficiency of the Holy Bible. On the other hand, in those churches which place great importance upon the full acceptance of certain creeds and confessions there is much less actual agreement than one would expect to find. Liberty in the former churches has not led to undisciplined anarchy of belief. Authority in the latter churches has not destroyed freedom. Within the framework of the essentials of Christian faith there is room for diversity of thinking and conviction. True unity will not be won by careless compromises with the truth of the gospel. Neither will it come through the imposition of a comprehensive dogmatic system. This is an application of the testimony of the Apostle Paul, that we must bring all things into captivity for Christ, but that Christ alone sets us free.

The same may be said of Christian worship. As one travels from country to country and visits many different churches, he is amazed by the numerous variations in liturgies, hymns, physical postures, customs, and underlying ideas which are included in Christian worship. An Orthodox churchman in the service of certain Reformed churches would fear he was attending an academic exercise. A Baptist at a Mar Thoma liturgy might at first sight think he was witnessing superstitious rites. An urbane Anglican at a village church in Africa, or even in the southern states of America, would be shocked by what he considered excessive emotion and "bad taste." But the Christian of the village church might be merely bored by the dignity and "good taste" of the worship of the city church. Extreme differences of worship-forms are found within some denominations without disrupting the unity of those communions. Is there not room in the one Church for wide varieties of practice in the adoration of

God? For beneath all the exterior forms of ritual and action which distinguish one type of Christian worship from another there is a common foundation which is uniquely and unmistakably Christian. This foundation is made up of such universally recognized elements as the reading of the Scriptures, preaching, the Holy Communion, praying and singing hymns of praise in the name of Jesus Christ.

Still another range of diversity among and within the churches concerns matters of moral and ethical judgment. Here it is a most precarious task to define with precision what kind of behavior is Christian and what is not. Obviously all are agreed on the Ten Commandments and the commandment of love. But how much agreement is there on the following questions: May a Christian serve in an army? Can a Christian admit divorce and the remarriage of divorced persons? Is a Christian allowed to drink wine or smoke tobacco? May a church accept financial aid from a government? Some Christians dismiss certain of these questions with hardly a thought. For others they are matters of the gravest importance. Are these legitimate diversities within the Church, or valid causes for division?

The catalogue of diverse teachings and practices could be drawn out to much greater length. But these are sufficient to show how much variety exists at present within the Church and within the various communions, and how little actual danger there is that the visible Church could ever become so uniform as some Christians fear.

If these many diversities in the Church are not only tolerable but even desirable for the well-being of the Church, is there any reason why divisions should arise at all? Ideally the answer is No. But divisions by the score have plainly arisen, and we must try to understand the causes of them.

Certainly we should be doing an injustice to the facts of history if we declared that all divisions, being bad, must have come about simply through a sectarian spirit and the unwarranted self-confidence of a group or church that it alone possessed the truth of the gospel. Some have, but not all. Many divisions have been caused because of the heroic work and prophetic witness of persons who desired only to serve the gospel humbly, and to introduce reforms into the Church according to the gospel. And yet what they held to be their fidelity to the Lord made it impossible for them to do otherwise. "Here I stand," declared Martin Luther, knowing that his firm position would lead to his being ejected from the Church of Rome. To have withdrawn the charges he made against the corruptions of the Church of Rome just for the sake of preserving its unity would have been for him an act of treason against God. Neither could John Calvin in Switzerland nor Thomas Cranmer in England finally retract the protest that each had made in the name of the gospel. Nor could Roger Williams in seventeenth-century America sell his faith for the sake of unity in an intolerant established Puritan Church. Nor did John Wesley feel directed by the Holy Spirit to leave his thousands of faithful followers without ministers in order to remain obedient to the rules of the Church of England. All were convinced on the basis of the Bible that the principles for which they contended were indispensable to the welfare of the Church.

In that same spirit of conviction today there are faithful Christians who believe that they cannot repair the divisions of history by bringing about church unions based upon easy compromises. As the Orthodox sees the tradition and teaching of his church, as the Anglican sees the ministry and sacraments, as the Lutheran or Calvinist sees his confession of faith, as the Baptist sees his insistence upon believer's baptism alone—as all these see the distinctive features of their churchly identity, they are fundamental elements of Christianity itself, which cannot be traded off in the name of unity. For unity must never be sought by neglecting Christian truth, as though unity were more important than truth. Christ who is the truth is also the one in whom there is unity.

Is there any escape from this perplexing situation, in which the members of certain churches are torn between a longing to be at one with all their fellow Christians and an inability to attain that visible oneness without forfeiting what they believe to be divinely given truth? This is precisely the dilemma in which Christians find themselves today. There is no known answer which is easy to apply. That is why the movement of the churches for visible unity requires so much patience, wisdom, love, and suffering. As one of the reports of a conference of the World Council of Churches puts it: "The point at which we are unable to renounce the things that divide us, because we believe that obedience to God himself compels us to stand fast—this is the point at which we come together to ask for mercy and light. So what we believe to be our 'faithfulness' must bring us together at the foot of the Cross." *

What shall we say then of the diversities and differences among the churches which do not affect essential parts of the gospel? Such differences as represent the natural variations in human dispositions and cultural patterns

* Faith and Order Report, Evanston Assembly, 1954.

should simply show forth the richness of the Church and the power of Jesus Christ to draw all sorts and conditions of men into his fellowship. But often there are groups of Christians who seize one particular diversity of doctrine or worship or ethical judgment and turn that into a principle of exclusion. They claim that any others who cannot agree with them on this point can no longer have fellowship with them. They thereby begin to make an idol of this peculiarity and to worship it. They seem to say to the world that Christ has given unity to the Church, but that this unity is found only where there is agreement with themselves. Hence, in effect, they think of themselves as being the only true and faithful Christians. The essence of this divisive spirit is called sectarianism.

Is it possible to draw a distinction between divisions which are caused by the idolizing of certain diversities that have been treated as absolute, and divisions which result from the genuine desire to be faithful to the known will of God? Here we are asking the deepest question of all. What is the clear and explicit authority of the Church where matters of truth and falsehood are involved? We reply, the Bible, of course. Yes, the Bible; but how interpreted? By the inner testimony of the Holy Spirit? By faith and reason? By the teaching power of the Church? The plain and sometimes distressing fact is that even among those who have the utmost belief in the Bible as the revelation of God's Word, there is no unanimity. And it is presumptuous indeed, if not perilous, for any one group to decide that it alone knows the will of God in accurate detail. This is nevertheless the assumption of those who are convinced that they only, of all the persons and congregations which profess faith in Jesus Christ, have the truth.

32

For example, there are some bodies of Christians which hold that the Church can be true to God's will only when it is independent of the state; some which insist upon one and only one view of the Bible and its authority; some which claim to have restored to perfection the organization of the New Testament Church; some which exclude all who disagree, for instance, on the immorality of smoking and drinking; still others who believe that baptism can be practiced by only one mode—total immersion in the water. Whether such reasons can warrant the division of the Church must be decided only after a strong affirmative has been given to the question: Does the Bible give overriding, unshakable support to them?

The kind of divisions with which we are concerned are not, therefore, the mere variations to be found in worship, teaching, and practice. We are thinking instead of those schisms within the one great Church which separate Christians into opposed, self-sufficient, and sometimes hostile communions, confessions, or denominations. For example, so far as their relations to one another are concerned, Lutherans, Baptists, and Anglicans are all radically divided. In only rare instances are members of any one of these confessions permitted to share in the Lord's Supper in a church of one of the other two. Wherever they have churches in the same village or city, there is little outward sign that their members have a bond of unity in Jesus Christ. Admitting certain exceptions, it is generally true to say that in their existence as church bodies, whether locally, nationally, or on a world-wide scale, they are concerned almost exclusively with the well-being of their own people and institutions. The same can be said of other denominations as well. This is division at its deepest and worst, when Christians in the same locality say in effect, "We have no need of you who are in other churches." It is almost better to have tensions and conflicts among Christians than such cold indifference, for in conflict at least there is personal encounter.

Yet there are exceptions, and very important ones, which demonstrate that the unity of Christ's people can be obscured but not destroyed. It often happens that, despite the official barriers of church doctrine and rules which separate them, individual Christians of different churches are closer to each other than to members of their own churches. Lines of common agreement and purpose cut across confessional boundaries. Often these surprising agreements are found in the realm of religious thought and viewpoint. More often they have little to do with theology. The common loyalties provoked by culture, nationality, social class, language, and local citizenship may do more to knit Christians together in one fellowship than the bonds of denominational tradition, doctrine, and order.

This mention of the way social and cultural factors cut across the boundaries of denominations reminds us that such factors have also been highly instrumental in bringing about church divisions in the past and perpetuating them in the present. The trouble is that Christians like to think that any divisions in which their own churches took part, or from which their churches have derived, were entirely of a doctrinal nature. Theology is more respectable in the church than sociology or economics. It is preferable to say that a certain denomination came into existence in order to keep the gospel pure instead of admitting that it was due to a strong sense of nationalism. But this does not explain why churches bearing the names of European countries are still found in America, Africa, and Asia. Money also plays its part. In some regions which were until recently regarded as "mission fields," church unions are being sought. For some churches it seems satisfying to the conscience if certain doctrinal arguments against the union can be raised in such a way as to conceal the fear that they will receive less money from the mission boards after a union. If one reads carefully the true history of the Church, he will see that time and again the divisions have been caused, not only by contending for truth, but by contention between bishops for personal power, by frictions between Christians of different nationalities, by struggle for the possession of property or for the rule of nations, by the assertion of superiority by members of one race over those of another, by the clannishness of small groups, and similar nondoctrinal factors.

The crucial question today is: What do Christians really think of the divisions of the Church? If they cheerfully accept them, if they deny the evil of division by saying that a "unity of the Spirit" is enough, or if they do no more than admit halfheartedly that division is bad and that unity would be a "good thing to have," there can be little hope that the efforts of farsighted prophets of Christian unity will bear much fruit. But if Christians regard division as sin which is hindering the work of God in Christ for the reconciling of persons to one another and to himself, they will have strong cause to fight against everything which divides the one Church into many parties.

To say that division is the result of sin is not the same as accusing all persons who have taken part in acts of division of being willful sinners. As we have seen, nearly all the men who have been involved in the breaking off of new Christian movements which became denominations were contending for the truth and purity of the Church. They desired, not division, but inner reform. Often they abhorred division. More than fifteen hundred years ago, the great patriarch and preacher John Chrysostom of Constantinople was anguished over party strife and political intrigue in the Church. Preaching on Ephesians 4:16, he declared: "Nothing will so avail to divide the Church as the love of authority. Nothing so provokes God's anger as the division of the Church." When one considers the other terrible sins which anger God—idolatry, adultery, murder—one wonders whether the saint was not exaggerating. But he meant the words literally. *Nothing* angers God so much as division. Why? Because the Church is the instrument created by God for extending the salvation wrought by Jesus Christ to all generations in all the world. And divisions hinder and frustrate that saving purpose of God.

So in the present century the movement for Christian unity has been motivated as much by abhorrence of the sin of division as by aspiration after the blessing of unity. This note was sounded at the first conference on Faith and Order, Lausanne, 1927, by Peter Ainslie of the Disciples of Christ in America. He declared: "Because the Church is a brotherhood, division is sin. To claim that this or that is *the* Church and others are 'schismatics' or 'the sects' or 'the denominations' is but playing with words in order to dodge repentance." Strong words, but necessary, if Christians are to be brought to a recognition of the sinfulness of division and the need for repentance and healing by God's mercy and power.

More recently the sinfulness of division has been interpreted in the light of the missionary obligation of the

Church. It is the duty of the Church on earth to proclaim the gospel. But the gospel is not merely a promise of the salvation of individual persons. It tells of the reconciliation of these persons with one another in the community of faith. By the death and resurrection of Jesus Christ they have been made at one with each other. This is precisely the message which the non-Christians of our time are hungry to hear and believe, that God in Christ can overcome the enmities and hostilities among men. Now comes the Church and announces reconciliation in Christ. But the non-Christian, seeing how little evidence there is of reconciliation among the Christians themselves, is either confused or amused, depending upon whether he is serious or skeptical about the Christian message. This very grave matter was emphasized at the World Council of Churches' Assembly in 1954, when a report said of division, "It is sinful because it obscures from men the sufficiency of Christ's atonement, inasmuch as the Gospel of reconciliation is denied in the very lives of those who proclaim it." Commenting on this idea, Bishop Newbigin of the Church of South India wrote: "No one who has shared in the task of seeking to commend Christ to those of other faiths can escape the shame of that denial. . . . To say that the Church must be one in order that the world may believe is to summon one another to a return to the source of the Church's being in Christ himself. . . . And when we allow the living Christ to do His atoning work in us, to break down our divisions and to knit us into one, we are by that very fact given a new power to go out to the world to invite all men to share in the atonement which is for all." *

---

* *The Household of God* (London, 1953), p. 150.

chapter **3**

Dividing and Healing in the Church's History

THE SKEPTICAL French philosopher Voltaire remarked: "The shameful quarrels of divided Christians have done more mischief under religious pretences, made more bad blood, and shed more human blood, than all the political contentions which have laid waste France and Germany under pretence of maintaining the balance of Europe." With the deepest sorrow and shame we must admit much truth in his charge.

Often it is said that the long history of the Church has been simply a sad story of schism. Church history is frequently taught as though this were the whole of the truth. But there is an opposite and equally valid way of regarding this complex history—as a continuous struggle by faithful Christians to restore and preserve the unity of the Church. We hear much about the movement for unity in the present time. The fact is that this movement had its origin in the time of the New Testament.

We have seen already that divisiveness entered the fellowship of the followers of Jesus from the outset. Even the disciples quarreled in the presence of Jesus as to which was the greatest. After the Christian Church was baptized with the Spirit and inaugurated at Pentecost, the very diverse kinds of believers fell naturally into groups and parties. There were no open breaks; no denominations formed. But we can read between the lines of the Acts of the Apostles and Paul's letters and see that the reason why there is strong insistence upon the God-given blessing of unity is that the threatening divisions had to be combated.

Even in the first century clouds of heresy which threatened to suffocate the Church were gathering. This was the religious movement known as Gnosticism. In some forms it had the effect of denying God as Creator of the world and Jesus Christ as the Word of God made flesh. It further weakened the biblical conception of sin, and turned salvation into a fantastic scheme which had no particular use for the cross of Christ. This was a corrupting movement of major proportions, and a terrible danger to the truth and unity of the Church. In three actions of prime importance the Church reacted effectively to clarify its doctrine and to defend its unity. It agreed on the canon of books which make up the Bible and submitted itself to their authority; it fixed the essentials of the faith in what became the Apostles' Creed as the profession of faith at baptism; and it regularized the episcopal structure of the ministry.

This was not the only divisive force in that period, which is usually given the optimistic but inaccurate name of the "time of the undivided Church."

From the second century onward there were several conflicting and divisive movements in Christianity. In the fourth century the Church experienced its greatest inner tensions over the question of the true interpretation of the Person of Jesus Christ. The followers of various theological leaders formed separate parties. The question, so simple to pose but never quite possible to answer, was: In what manner can Jesus Christ be said to be both God and man? This was not a matter of haphazard speculation. It was and is of fundamental importance for the Christian faith.* How could the unity of the Church be secured in the face of these strong tensions?

The initiative was taken by the Emperor Constantine, who had just made Christianity the favored religion of the Roman Empire. He had hoped that Christianity, with its doctrine of unity in Christ, would be the cement of the empire. Instead he found himself trying to patch the cracks in the structure of the Church. To the town of Nicaea (now in Turkey) in 325 he called 318 bishops to assemble in a great council. Appearing before them as their convener, he declared, in the imagined words of a modern dramatist, Dorothy Sayers: "To me, your fellow servant, any dissension within the Church appears a thing as dreadful as war and perhaps more difficult to bring to an end." Even though this First Ecumenical Council did not end dissension, it fixed the pattern for that which is now almost universally accepted as the Christian doctrine of Christ, and which was incorporated in what we know as the Nicene Creed.

By the year 787 no less than seven great councils had been held, not only to clarify questions of doctrine and discipline, but to manifest and preserve the unity of the Church against division. Historians disagree as to how

* The parties and their teachings are described by Bishop Neill in *Who Is Jesus Christ?* (World Christian Books), chap. 5.

truly representative these councils were and how effectively they kept the unity. From our modern standpoint it may seem that they were nearly as much concerned to describe the errors of their enemies as to define the truth of the gospel. The terrible word "anathema," meaning accursed and excommunicated, was hurled against numerous actual and alleged enemies of the faith. But despite these negative decisions, it is significant to note that the doctrinal definitions of these councils did much to shape our Christian faith and practice.

It was during these centuries that the tension was increasing between Eastern Orthodoxy and Western Catholicism. The causes of the tension were a tangle of theology, politics, custom, and personalities, too complex for analysis here. They ranged from little disputes as to the eating of milk products during Lent to the question of whether the Holy Spirit "proceeds" from the Father *and* the Son, or from the Father alone; from disputes over the use of ikons (sacred pictures) and images in Christian devotion to the political tension between Rome and Constantinople, and the increasing claim of the Roman papacy to absolute ecclesiastical power. In 1054 the Pope excommunicated the Eastern Church; later the schism became bitterly real to the people, after the nominally Christian Crusaders of the West had slaughtered their Eastern brothers in the battle of Constantinople, 1204.

The Christian conscience was once more outraged by such horrible division, and again attempts were made to reconcile the estranged parties. The Council of Lyons (France) assembled in 1274, and it seemed for a while that union had been restored. But unfortunately the foundations of agreement were not carefully laid. The Eastern delegates returned home to meet a rejection of the terms

41

they had agreed to, which included submission to the Pope. A second attempt at Ferrara (Italy) in 1438, and Florence in 1439, also came to naught. So that even today this great breach has never been repaired.

Meanwhile Roman Catholic unity itself was threatened by the rival advocates of the papacy or of councils as the supreme authority of the church. In fact, for nearly forty years there were two popes at once, in Rome and in Avignon (France) respectively, each claiming legal right. The Council of Constance (Switzerland) in 1415 brought this so-called "Babylonian Captivity" to an end. The same council sentenced one of the earliest reformers, John Huss of Bohemia, who anticipated the Reformation by more than a century, to be burned at the stake.

The Reformation of the sixteenth century marked the beginning of the modern era of the Christian Church. Unfortunately but unavoidably this era began with a "chain reaction" of church divisions. At least ten of the great denominational families had their origin in the Reformation.

Roman Catholics believe generally that the Reformation had only one meaning: schism, or even heresy. But, as we have noted, the reformers themselves treasured unity and deplored division. Yet they knew that an outward, institutional unity was of little value so long as the leaders of that ecclesiastical institution actually prevented the preaching of the gospel, forbade the reading of the Bible, and winked at gross sins among its clergy.

It must never be assumed that Christians of the sixteenth century were either contented with or unconcerned about the new divisions. Their desire to restore unity quickly, but on the basis of a true reformation of the Church, was manifest in the frequent attempts which were

42

made to heal the breach. The greatest scholar of the time, Erasmus, strove for conciliation through his influence on the intellectuals of the Church. "We have had enough of quarrels," he wrote in 1533; "perhaps sheer weariness may bring us together in concord." But Erasmus failed to understand the depth of the doctrinal divisions.

As Lutheranism spread over Europe, negotiations were held in hopes of restoring agreement. At Ratisbon (Regensburg, Germany) in 1541 the leading Protestant thinkers Calvin, Bucer, and Melanchthon tried to agree with the Roman Catholic representatives on the meaning of such questions as justification by faith, the Holy Communion or Mass, and the papacy. But such agreement simply could not be achieved. The Church as well as the nations was by that time shaken to the foundations by the spreading Reformation. There seemed to be little hope left for reconciliation. Then the Roman hierarchy summoned church leaders of Europe to a great council at the town of Trent (Italy) in 1545. Here began the Counter Reformation. The dogmas of the Roman Church were given definition in such a way that the principles upon which Protestantism rested were totally excluded. Even today these doctrinal definitions, which determine Roman Catholic teaching, are among the main barriers to reconciliation with Protestants. The official position of that church with respect to reunion is that all non-Romans must submit to papal authority and accept all the dogmas of the Roman Catholic Church.

Almost as difficult as restoring unity with the Roman Church was the task of effecting unity among the Protestants themselves. By the middle of the sixteenth century there were three main blocs of continental Protestant churches: Lutheran, Zwinglian, and Calvinistic. Outside these was the movement of the Anabaptists, who insisted on believers' baptism only, separation from control by the state, and pacifism. The leaders of the three large groups sought agreement among themselves. The one point on which they agreed too readily was that the Anabaptists and similar "pests," as Luther called them, should be persecuted and extinguished. Despite some progress, they unfortunately failed in the first effort and happily failed in the second.

The first effort to unite the forces of Protestant churches was the conference held at Marburg (Germany) in 1529, where Luther met Huldrich Zwingli of Zurich, along with other colleagues. Present also was Martin Bucer of Strassburg, called justly "the most zealous exponent of the ideal of church unity of his age." Political as well as theological issues were at stake when these Germans and Swiss came together. Much concord was indeed secured. On fourteen of fifteen propositions they agreed. But when they came to the question of how Christ is present in the Lord's Supper, Zwingli and Luther could not agree. Luther believed that the words of Jesus, "This is my body," should be taken literally as applied to the bread. Zwingli said that Jesus meant, "This signifies my body." The disagreement went deep, and it was coupled with their opposed views of political tactics in advancing the Reformation. They parted on Luther's famous, tragic words: "You are of another spirit than we."

In a more mellow atmosphere, an agreement on the Lord's Supper was achieved at Wittenberg in 1536 by Bucer and Luther's friend Melanchthon. Then Bucer found that he could not secure the agreement of Zwingli's successor, Bullinger, in Switzerland. The "Wittenberg

Concord" remained, however, a strong force making for unity.

John Calvin, who was bringing the Reformation to fruition in Geneva, now attempted to mediate between Wittenberg and Zurich. He failed with the German Lutherans, but succeeded in bringing together the Swiss reformed Christians in agreement on the "Zurich Consensus." Calvin then sought to bring about a great council of European Protestants which could settle once and for all the doctrinal issues which divided them. The plan was shared by Thomas Cranmer, Archbishop of Canterbury, and by Melanchthon. But it came to naught. Calvinism and Lutheranism hardened into rocklike dogmatic systems, and so they prevailed in the seventeenth century. The one successful agreement in this time of separation was the decision of the French Reformed Church at Charenton in 1631 to admit Lutherans to their Communion services.

Advocates of union were not, however, lacking. The Lutheran pastor with the pen name "Meldenius" coined in 1626 his famous motto: "In things necessary, unity; in things not necessary, liberty; in all things, charity." Could not churches unite on the essentials of faith?

A leading German Lutheran theologian, George Calixtus, at this time preached unity on the basis of the faith and practice of the early church. Like many before and after him, he sought unity on the basis of the ancient words of Vincent of Lerins, "What has been believed always, everywhere, and by all people."

Some of the most consecrated work for unity on the European continent was done in the seventeenth century by a Scotsman, John Dury. As a young man he vowed that he would dedicate his whole life to Christian unity.

He never faltered in that mission for his remaining fifty years. He tried to draw the churches into a great conference on unity, but without success. Despite these and other remedial efforts, a way could not be found at that time for the healing of the deep wounds of division in the body of Christ. The individual prophets of unity lacked the support of the leaders and of the ordinary members of the churches.

It was in the late sixteenth and seventeenth centuries that storms of division swirled through the British churches. Anglicans were torn between their Catholic heritage and the newly recovered values of the biblical Reformation. Calvinistic theology and presbyterian government were advocated by the Puritans. The Scots had already accepted the tenets of Calvin as mediated by John Knox. Then Independency, which stressed local congregational self-rule, increased in strength. Baptists and Quakers bore their distinctive witness. And, as usually happens, these diverse religious movements became entangled in opposing political forces. "It is a pitiful case with the poor afflicted Church of Christ," moaned a leading exponent of unity in Britain, Richard Baxter, "that almost all her Members cry out against Division, and yet cause and increase it while they speak against it." Contention among the Christians of England over the question of whether the churches should be episcopalian or presbyterian in order was not a simple dispute over alternative forms of government. It concerned the true nature of the Church itself. Was Christ's Church by its very essence episcopal in form? The question was prominent then as it is today in church union discussions. Then as now there was no full agreement among Anglicans with regard to it. It is known that leading Anglican theologians and bishops of the early sev-

46

enteenth century favored full communion with the Reformed churches of Europe. A few Reformed ministers, though lacking episcopal ordination, were even appointed to Anglican parishes. The saintly Bishop Lancelot Andrewes gladly recognized the nonepiscopal churches as churches.

The Westminster Assembly of 1643 marked the temporary victory of the party favoring presbyterianism. Episcopacy was abolished by act of the British Parliament, which was then controlled by forces opposing monarchy. But with the restoration of the king in 1660 the strong advocates of episcopacy returned to power. The tables were turned when in 1662 the Act of Uniformity ejected 1,760 independent and presbyterian ministers from parish churches, and reintroduced episcopalians. Throughout this time of crisis, leaders on both sides tried to maintain harmony and unity in the church; but history shows that an almost irreconcilable division separated the two parties. The Presbyterians inevitably became a denomination outside the Church of England.

Although the ways of these Christian parties in England were diverging at the end of the century, there was a remarkable converging of relations between the English and the continental churches. Between Archbishop Wake of Canterbury and leading churchmen of Holland, France, Germany, and Switzerland there were frequent communications. Few persons challenged seriously the right of Christians, whether episcopal or not, to share the Holy Communion in churches of other countries. The German court-preacher D. E. Jablonski even set forth at the opening of the eighteenth century a plan of union for all Evangelical churches in Prussia, based upon the episcopate to be introduced by Anglicans. And when the Anglican Society for Promoting Christian Knowledge desired to extend its mission to South India, there was little hesitation in supporting two Lutherans, Ziegenbalg and Plütschau, who had been sent to that country by the Danish Mission in 1705. A century later the Anglican Church Missionary Society also sent out German Lutheran ministers as their first missionaries.

After these promising beginnings, the eighteenth century showed steady decline in interest in church unity. On the continent of Europe there seemed to be hope of advance toward unity through the influential work of Count von Zinzendorf. Although his followers, the Moravian Brethren, became in time a separate body, he was himself a man of deepest "catholic spirit," and did much to persuade men that Christian unity was better served by earnest prayer than by clever negotiations. The common experience of personal salvation by Christ should be the basis of unity.

Zinzendorf's major effect upon English church life, though indirect, was the conversion of John Wesley, the most important Englishman of the century. Wesley was primarily an evangelist, and an incomparably effective one. It is true that his Methodist movement led at last to a new schism in the Church of England, but this was wholly contrary to his will. He claimed no exclusive truth for his teaching, which for him was simply the universal Christian faith.

The century closed on a scene which foretold the coming interplay of Christian mission and Christian unity. In 1795 the London Missionary Society was constituted as a nondenominational sending society. "Here are Episcopalians, Methodists, Presbyterians, and Independents all united in one Society," declared a speaker at its founding;

"Behold us here assembled with one accord to attend the funeral of bigotry."

As one reviews the history of the nineteenth century from the point of view of Christian unity, he can see that it was a steady progress in preparation for the great unity movement of the twentieth century. The hand of God was directing the actions of men. Those good Christians had no more clear vision of what God had in store for the churches than we have today. But they, like us, knew that the unitive power of Jesus Christ made sectarian divisions intolerable. This was the era of the great new missionary thrust of the Protestant churches of Europe and North America to the peoples of Africa and Asia and Oceania. And the lesson was soon learned that there is little harmony between the Church's evangelistic mission and denominational schisms.

This was also the period when many interdenominational activities were being fostered, in particular the various Bible Societies and Sunday School Unions. Christians discovered that the task of education, as well as evangelism, demands mutual co-operation.

In England, Scotland, and North America there had sprung up a bewildering variety of small denominations. The great Presbyterian, Methodist, and Lutheran church families each suffered from internal divisions. These began to mend themselves through numerous mergers of smaller units. Their own family quarrels were being settled before they could look toward closer fellowship with other church families.

In 1809 a movement for comprehensive union took form in America under the leadership of Thomas Campbell. In the words of his *Declaration and Address,* which sound so modern to our ears today, he condemned divisions, commended unity in Christ, and called for a return to the simplicity of New Testament Christianity. "Unite with us in the common cause of simple evangelical Christianity," he called. As to the ground of unity, "Nothing ought to be received into the faith or worship of the Church, or to be made a term of communion among Christians, that is not as old as the New Testament." Despite this noble intent, the irony of the story is that these "Disciples of Christ" became in time another denomination and even suffered their own inner discords.

In 1817, just three hundred years after Luther's break with Rome, the Lutheran and Reformed churches of Prussia came into a new union. In the succeeding years this spread to several other German states. This union has lasted to the present day. But it has been severely criticized because it was planned, and indeed coerced, by the Prussian king. Doctrinal and liturgical differences were ignored. Even today the inner strains have not all been eased. The elements which are Reformed can still be distinguished from those which are Lutheran. Yet the union has held together. Many of its members are trying to make it still stronger with due attention to doctrine.

The effects of this bold union were felt on the far side of the Atlantic Ocean. Lutheranism had splintered in the new America according to the national backgrounds of immigrants. These had encouraged few relationships with Christians of other denominations. But it was a Lutheran, S. S. Schmucker, whose voice was the strongest for general unity among the American churches. In 1839 he published his ambitious plan for "the Apostolic Protestant Church," to be based upon the fundamentals of faith held in common by all. This would have been more of a close federation of existing denominations than an organic union.

The plan was never considered seriously by the churches. However, it did much to form the dominating conception of Christian unity in the minds of American Protestants for many decades to come. This conception stressed the need for retaining denominational identity within a cooperative federation.

Schmucker's strong viewpoint was shared in England by Angell James and in Scotland by Thomas Chalmers. These men were largely instrumental in establishing in 1846 the Evangelical Alliance. This was an organization not for church union but for the unity of Christian persons despite their denominational membership. Yet its influence upon the thinking of countless Christians about Christian unity has been immense. It was, indeed, the first world-wide organization of its kind. And it continues to be a force for unity and evangelism through its conferences and publications.

Churches of the Anglican Communion during the nineteenth century both consolidated their own churches and sought a ground for unity with others. The first development found expression in the Lambeth Conference to which all Anglican bishops were invited, which met first in 1867. The second took the form of a formula for unity. On what basis could Anglicans consider unity with other Christian bodies? The answer arose in the mind of the Episcopalian prophet of unity in America, W. R. Huntington. Four points were irreducible essentials of the church, he wrote in 1870. These were formulated and later adopted by the Lambeth Conference of 1888, since which time they have been known as the "Lambeth Quadrilateral." No discussion of possible union involving Anglicans can ignore these four essentials: "(1) The Holy Scriptures of the Old and New Testaments as containing all things

51

necessary to salvation, and as being the rule and ultimate standard of faith. (2) The Apostles' Creed, as the Baptismal Symbol; and the Nicene Creed as the sufficient statement of the Christian faith. (3) The two Sacraments ordained by Christ himself—Baptism and the Supper of the Lord—ministered with unfailing use of Christ's words of institution and of the elements ordained by Him. (4) The Historic Episcopate, locally adapted in the methods of its administration to the varying needs of the nations and peoples called of God into the unity of His Church."

Meanwhile the missionary movement throughout the world was being blessed with much success. Churches began to grow in localities where Christ's name had never before been spoken. How could this universal mission be effective if the persons responsible for it worked in isolation from one another? The pioneer in India, William Carey, had suggested in 1806 the plan of a world missionary conference. This dream was not realized until 1910. But the interdenominational American Board of Commissioners for Foreign Missions was already in 1838 proposing the principle of "comity" in missionary work, so as to avoid competition. And a continuing series of widely representative conferences on missions began in the middle of the century. The first general Christian conference in India met at Calcutta in 1855. By 1872 larger gatherings were being held at ten-year intervals. A similar meeting was held in Japan the same year, and in China in 1877. Voices were being raised in protest against the importing of alien denominational divisions along with the gospel. Proposals were also heard for making the oneness of the Church of Christ a visible reality in lands where it was growing up in new forms.

In Britain and America the denominations at this time

considered it a notable success whenever they brought into reunion two or more separate bodies of one family. In India, however, the first major union of unlike denominations was achieved in 1908. The Presbyterians and Congregationalists agreed then to live and worship together as one body called the South India United Church. This eventually was one of the churches which joined to form the Church of South India. Its formation at the beginning of the twentieth century marked the time when some 142,000 Christians began to reap the harvest of unity which had been planted and nurtured in many fields of the world during the nineteenth century.

Chapter 4

Half a Century of Rapid Advance

THE BIBLE is sometimes described as a retelling of
"the mighty acts of God." The creation of the world, the
calling of Abraham, the covenant, the exodus, the preser-
vation of the faithful remnant, the sending of Jesus Christ
to die and rise again, the gift of the Holy Spirit, the life
of the Church: so has God acted mightily. But he did not
stop acting at Pentecost. We can assert that the sweeping
movement for Christian unity represents one of God's
mighty acts. Therefore the best way to deal with this
movement in the twentieth century is to recite some of
these acts as we have known them.

Great moments of this movement have been the peri-
odic world Christian conferences held from 1910 onward,
with delegates attending from many parts of the world.
The conferences need to be known as background for the
present situation, but in themselves they are less important than what has happened to persons attending them
and to persons influenced by them. Prejudices have been
abolished. Doctrinal variations have been explained and

understood. Strange or little-known church customs have been appreciated, so that the diversity of the Church has been better esteemed. Traditional treasures of worship have been shared. And the vision of the Church of Christ in its wholeness, obedience, and unity has been held before faithful eyes which otherwise would not have beheld it. In all this, a new climate of opinion has evolved in which suspicion, jealousy, and bigotry have no place.

We have made it clear in foregoing pages that the divisions of the churches, however disagreeable they may be in the settled "Christian" nations of Europe and America, are simply intolerable in those predominantly non-Christian lands, where the newer churches live on the frontier of the faith. Abundant witness has been borne by Christians of Asia especially that the sectarian schisms within Christianity disillusion or frighten off many persons who respond positively to the preaching of the gospel. It was this message of the need for visible unity which certain Asian delegates brought to the World Missionary Conference held at Edinburgh in 1910. In the assembly of 1,300 delegates there were less than 20 Asians. Their spokesmen were V. S. Azariah of India and Cheng Ching-yi of China. But many a missionary from the West joined in this call for unity, stating his beliefs in the conference sessions.

It is impossible to exaggerate the significance of the Edinburgh Conference. It marked a new era in the history of the Church. What had been occasionally desired in the past was now permitted to be a reality. This was due both to the growing appreciation of that fact that Christians in the whole world belong to one another, and also to the technical developments which made rapid correspondence and travel possible.

The man who more than any other was responsible for

bringing this conference together was John R. Mott. It is difficult to think of any man in the entire history of the Church whose life and kind of service resembled Mott's. He was an evangelist of towering stature, but not a theologian or original thinker. He became one of the foremost church leaders of the world, but remained a layman. He was an American Methodist, but was given highest honors by the Orthodox and other churches in virtually every country of the world where Christians are to be found. His primary devotion was to the cause of enlisting Christian students for Jesus Christ's service. In 1889 he had helped to organize the Student Volunteer Movement, and in 1895 the World's Student Christian Federation. He never tired of ranging over the world, challenging students to give their lives to missionary service by holding forth the goal of "the evangelization of the world in this generation." From the time of his young manhood his name was also identified with the Young Men's Christian Association. He helped to develop this as a world-wide youth movement of incalculable value both to the Christian mission and the unity of the Church. As though these fields of service were not enough, Mott undertook one of his most important tasks in 1908 when he began planning for the Missionary Conference at Edinburgh. It was he who naturally was chosen to be its chairman.

Mott chose as executive secretary of the conference a young leader of the Student Christian Movement in Scotland, J. H. Oldham. Oldham himself became one of the few really indispensable leaders of what has come to be known as the Ecumenical Movement. Writing a sensitive memoir on the occasion of Mott's death in 1955 at the age of eighty-nine, he pointed out that Mott's decision to have the purposes of the Edinburgh Conference carried out by a well-run continuation committee was a bold new plan which has had immense effect upon the unity movement. This was the first interdenominational and international organ brought into existence to serve the world mission of the Church. From this committee there evolved the present International Missionary Council, formed in 1921.

Despite the relatively slow means of travel available in the early years of this century, John R. Mott managed to visit and revisit numerous Asian countries. He always identified himself personally with the thinking and viewpoint of Asians. Oldham recalls that Mott was almost alone in persuading the Edinburgh preparatory committee that the Asian churches should be represented by their own people. He was directly responsible also for establishing various National Christian Councils, which he called his "first and greatest contributions" to the I.M.C.

While the Edinburgh Conference was primarily concerned with the new problems arising in the vast missionary work of the churches, it could not escape the related problem of church divisions. It was the agreed policy of the conference not to allow this problem to be discussed. To be sure, it was an explosive matter for which only a few minds were prepared. Unions within denominational families had been taking place for decades. But Edinburgh demonstrated the need to consider the more difficult state of interdenominational relations. For the first time in their lives, probably, many delegates faced in a personal, non-theoretical way the scandal of divisions at the Lord's Supper. No common service of Holy Communion was possible.

The pain of this experience was particularly acute for one man, and it caused him to become the originator of a mighty new force in Christian thinking. He was Charles H. Brent, a missionary to the Philippines and a bishop of the Episcopal Church in America. Bearing the weight of division in his heart throughout the conference, he nevertheless began to see opening before the churches a new and hopeful way to unity. What if there could take place a conference like this one, he thought, in which representatives of all the churches of the world could face together, frankly, charitably, and intelligently, the issues which really divide them! This would be a conference devoted to consideration of doctrines, beliefs, confessions—Faith—as well as polity, organization, and ministry—Order. With this idea in mind, he prayed fervently for God to guide him.

His own church responded positively to the plan which he described, even though its revolutionary newness evoked opposition from many. The Disciples of Christ and the Congregationalists in America concurred. A lawyer and leading Episcopal layman, Robert Gardiner, then past fifty, was named secretary of his church's new commission on Faith and Order. Until his death in 1926 he gave amazingly industrious, imaginative, and humble service to this new cause. That a movement involving the leading theologians and clergy of the world should be dependent upon the wisdom and energy of a layman is comparable to the similar position of Mott.

How preparations were made for the first World Conference on Faith and Order is an adventurous and fascinating story. Gardiner corresponded with many thousands of Christians throughout the world. The war of 1914–18 delayed but did not defeat the work. When peace came again, a delegation traveled throughout eastern Europe, enlisting the support of the leaders of Orthodox churches.

They even visited Rome and invited the Pope to send representatives, but this request was politely declined.

The first meeting of world-wide representation was held at Geneva in 1920. To be sure, it was not so fully representative as we expect such conferences to be today. Of the 70 churches involved, the great majority were in Europe and America. Asia was represented (with one exception, a Japanese) by non-Asian missionaries. From North Africa came only a few Orthodox prelates; from tropical Africa came no one. Apparently the time had not yet arrived when the "younger churches" were able to play their role. Under Bishop Brent's leadership the meeting drew up early plans for the long-anticipated conference. But seven more years of preparation were required before nearly 400 delegates from 108 churches gathered at Lausanne (Switzerland) in August, 1927.

Was the aim of the conference to make plans for the early unions of divided churches? Some thought so, but it was otherwise. Impetuous zealots for an organic union by the quickest and easiest means had to accept the limitation of discussion to general questions of doctrine, creeds, ministry, sacraments, and the theological meaning of the nature of the Church. Like others in ecumenical conferences still to come, they had to learn the basic lesson of responsible discussion: how to combine their zeal for church union with caution and a sense of the right time for pressing to decisions. The Bishop of Bombay, E. J. Palmer, who was then a pioneering figure in the negotiations which led to the formation of the Church of South India, wagged his great beard and warned: "This is a conference about truth, not about reunion. We engage in it because we desire the visible unity of Christ's Church on earth. Our disagreements about truth are considered by many to justify our disunion. Whether they do so or not, agreement about truth would be one of the firmest foundations for unity."

In contrast to those who urged hasty unions, the Orthodox delegates, who came in large numbers, were in a state of tension. They felt that the references in the reports to the reunion of churches were unwarranted and reckless. At Lausanne, as at subsequent conferences, the Orthodox felt compelled by their church's teachings to write a declaration of partial abstention from the main reports. This first experience of disappointment brought tears to the eyes of some of their delegates.

The final report of the conference insisted that it was "emphatically *not* attempting to define the conditions of future reunion." In so doing, it stated the kind of neutrality *in principle* toward specific church union schemes which ever since has been adhered to by the Faith and Order movement of the World Council of Churches. At the same time the report showed that concrete problems of church union cannot simply be ignored. It asserted, for example, a principle which has ever since been a guide in union negotiations: "In the order of life of a reunited Church" the elements of "episcopal, presbyteral and congregational systems of government" must all have "an appropriate place."

However neutral the official position of the conference might be, individual prophets of unity had their chance to speak. Once again it was Bishop Azariah of Dornakal who expressed the mind of many Indian Christians: "By our divisions, we not only waste our resources, but also diminish the Church's effectiveness for righteousness and purity in non-Christian lands. Unity, organic unity, is the only remedy. . . ." He continued: "We do not desire any one Church to absorb the others. We do not ask any one to deny its spiritual heritage, we cannot demand the severance of fellowship of any of these Churches with the Churches in Europe or America that have planted them. *But we must have one Church.* We want a Church of India, a Church which can be our spiritual home, a Church where the Indian religious genius can find natural expression, a living branch of the Holy, Catholic and Apostolic Church." In 1945 Azariah "died in faith, not having received what was promised." But twenty years and one month after he had made this speech, the Church of South India was inaugurated.

The dream of Bishop Brent, however, had been realized, his "promise" had been received, when in 1929 he died. By strange coincidence the end came while he was just passing through the city of Lausanne, and it was there that he was buried. Thereafter the mantle of leadership passed to another extraordinary man whom God had prepared for this task, William Temple, later Archbishop of Canterbury.

At Lausanne the need for continuing, deep-going studies of the things which divide Christians had been realized. These belong chiefly to the realm of theology. Many Christians are prejudiced against theology and doctrine. These only cause division, they say. Doctrine divides; service unites! It was the conviction of leaders of another parallel Christian movement that unity could best come, and perhaps only come, through the common co-operation of the churches in the fields of racial tension, economic justice, and international peace. This great effort, called the Conference on Life and Work, had already met in 1925 at Stockholm, entertained by its dynamic leader, Archbishop Söderblom of Sweden. Between the two movements was a kind of rivalry. The participants in both movements were soon going to understand, however, that theological problems cannot be so easily divorced from the rest of the church's task. Each movement decided to hold its second conference in Great Britain, at Edinburgh and Oxford respectively, in 1937.

William Temple was one of only a few delegates to Edinburgh, 1937, who had also attended (as an usher) the conference there in 1910. How different was the atmosphere of the meetings now! Instead of the earlier strangeness and stiffness of first acquaintance and the frequent doubts about the outcome of such a conference, there was now, twenty-seven years later, a mood of familiarity and confidence. Many of the delegates had been working together in previous meetings. The importance of such personal friendships across confessional lines must not be overlooked. "The fate of doctrines and ideas depends also on the behavior of the people who hold them," remarked a mission secretary.

The trend toward a more favorable proportion of delegates from the "younger churches" was also noticeable, if not yet sufficiently strong. Some 500 persons attended the conference. From China, Japan, and India came 25 delegates, but only 10 of them were nationals of those countries. The rest were Westerners, as were all those representing the churches of Africa.

These many theologians and church leaders dealt conscientiously with the difficult problems before them. How could they reconcile the deep divisions caused by differences in respect to the authority of the Holy Scriptures, the ministry, the sacraments, the meaning of divine grace, and the communion of saints? For the most part they were satisfied if they could come to a clear mutual understanding of what the various churches taught and believed. This is not so easy as one might think. A Baptist, for example, can study the Book of Common Prayer and the Thirty-nine Articles of the Church of England. But how can he really understand how an Anglican thinks and prays his faith; or how an Anglican honestly views the Baptist himself? All of our denominations have developed through the centuries not only systems of doctrine and worship, but also distinct attitudes, sentiments, and subconscious prejudices which are nearly impenetrable by someone of another church. So the Edinburgh report consisted inevitably of a good many statements *about* doctrines and practices on which there was either agreement or disagreement. It was unable to plunge deep into their meaning for the life and unity of the Church.

Nonetheless the recognition of the unity of the Church as something real, given by God in Christ, despite denominational divisions, was acknowledged more than ever before. As Temple expressed this insight in his sermon at the opening service: "Let us never forget that though the purpose of our meeting is to consider the causes of our divisions, yet what makes possible our meeting is our unity. We could not seek union if we did not already possess unity. Those who have nothing in common do not deplore their estrangement. It is because we are one in allegiance to one Lord that we seek and hope for the way of manifesting that unity in our witness to Him before the world."

It is necessary to point out that despite many sincere professions of unity in Christ on the part of the churches' delegates at Edinburgh, these 123 separate churches were not committed to one another by any official decisions. Neither were those represented at Oxford the same year in the Conference of the Life and Work movement. But

at these two meetings identical decisions of lasting importance were taken. They agreed to explore together the
possibility of forming a World Council of Churches. It was
hoped that such a Council would gather up the work done
by both movements and also constitute a co-operative
and consultative agency to which all the member churches
would commit themselves. This would be an innovation,
something unique, in the whole history of Christianity. It
would not be in any sense a legislating body. Each church
would maintain its complete independence and sover-
eignty. But it would provide both a forum for common
study and a channel for common activity in carrying out
the work of the churches throughout the world. Moreover,
it would inevitably bring the churches into such intimate
contact with each other that their divisions would cry out
all the louder for healing.

In 1938 at Utrecht (Holland) a conference was con-
vened to lay a solid foundation for the World Council.
The major work was done by Archbishop Temple, J. H.
Oldham, and two distinguished American churchmen,
William Adams Brown and Samuel McCrea Cavert. They
decided that membership in the Council would be open to
churches "which accept our Lord Jesus Christ as God and
Saviour." It was clear that this would be a Council of
Churches *of Christ*. It would not include religious bodies
which had any diffidence about confessing him.

What about the third great stream in this growing Ecumenical Movement, the International Missionary Council?
Was this to be included? Since its founding in 1921 the
I.M.C. had increased greatly in strength and influence. It
was an organization of world-wide scope which brought
into consultation and co-operation the missionary societies
and mission boards of many countries along with the

National Christian Councils and similar bodies in the younger churches. It had also carried through a series of significant conferences in continuity with Edinburgh, 1910. In the Holy City itself, Jerusalem, the second large meeting was held in 1928. Ten years later the third was convened at Tambaram near Madras, India.

There was no question now about adequate representation of "younger church" leaders in the I.M.C. They accounted for half the delegates at Tambaram. At this time the leaders of the I.M.C. considered and welcomed the plans being made in the same year by the Provisional Committee for the World Council of Churches. But they made no positive decision to enter into the formation of this new Council. Two main characteristics of the I.M.C. made it exceedingly difficult to reach such a decision. First, the I.M.C. was made up not of member churches but of Conferences of missionary societies and of Christian Councils. Second, there were well represented in its work a number of Christian groups which did not look favorably upon either the Faith and Order or the Life and Work movements. The essential task of the I.M.C., they felt, could be carried out better if it remained independent. Nevertheless, a bridge was formed when a joint committee between the two organizations was authorized, and William Paton of the I.M.C. staff was assigned to give part-time service to the World Council.

The Provisional Committee had decided that the World Council should be constituted formally at a great assembly in 1941. But even when this decision was made, it was clear to some persons that the horrible second world war was about to begin. This war isolated the German and eastern European churches from others with which they had had fellowship. It also caused dangerous tensions

65

within the churches of certain lands and threatened their existence. Never in modern times was there such need for true Christian unity. Thanks to God, the spirit of unity was not only maintained but even strengthened. One of the great heroes of the time, that immovable opponent of the Nazi menace, Bishop Berggrav of Oslo, Norway, declared: "In these last years we have lived more intimately with each other than in times when we could communicate with each other. We prayed together more, we listened together more to the Word of God, our hearts were together more." The frail structure of the new Council did not fall; it became firmer. At the close of the war in 1945, the churches sent their representatives to carry the formation of the Council to its completion.

The plans for the first Assembly were laid and formal invitations to membership were sent to the officers of churches around the world. One hundred and forty-seven of these responded, and sent 589 persons to Amsterdam in August, 1948. Assembled for worship and displaying by their dress all the diversities of nationality, culture, and confession, they heard the 83-year-old John R. Mott speak as was his habit of the future opportunities rather than the past accomplishments. The Reverend D. T. Niles, preaching the opening sermon, said, "The Christian witness recognizes no barriers and allows no partiality." At the opening business session the benign and dignified Pasteur Marc Boegner of France moved that the World Council of Churches be declared to be in existence. The unanimous vote was followed by ringing applause, then by reverent prayer led by the Archbishop of Canterbury.

What is this World Council which has come into being? This question is not so simple as some might think.

Is it one more interchurch organization for doing more

effectively what the churches would have to do singly? The Council's unprecedented program of relief and refugee service shows that it is this. And yet it is more. Is it a council for common study and discussion of important theological and social questions? It has proved to be this. And still more. For unlike all the other related organizations, the Council has an immediate reference to the meaning of the Church itself and its unity. The words of the Amsterdam Assembly Message which in an unplanned way became a kind of popular motto were these: "We intend to stay together." We, the 147 distinct churches, intend to keep this commitment to one another. It is this affirmation, which has been strengthened in the life of the Council year after year, which constitutes the historical uniqueness of it.

Having taken this bold step together in 1948, the churches were given a new sense of urgency about their obligation to overcome the ancient divisions between them. The Faith and Order movement, following the Amsterdam Assembly, became the Council's Commission on Faith and Order. Its peculiar task was defined as follows: "To proclaim the essential oneness of the Church of Christ and to keep prominently before the World Council and the Churches the obligation to manifest that unity and its urgency for the work of evangelism." In order to fulfill this primary function, the persons involved in the Commission's work are required to study deeply together the causes of division and the ways of unity, taking into account the work done by the churches themselves with respect to seeking closer fellowship or organic union.

The third World Conference on Faith and Order met in 1952 at Lund (Sweden), where the Commission's chairman, Archbishop Y. T. Brilioth of Uppsala, acted both as host and president. No longer distracted by the novelty of meeting as Christians from dozens of lands and churches, the delegates worked hard on three main areas of discussion. None of these can be legitimately neglected by those who take divisions seriously and desire unity earnestly.

The first was the Nature of the Church. This is the ancient question which, despite years of study and reflection, always seems new. What is essential to the Church as God wills it to be? Are various approximations of the "fullness" of the Church represented by different confessions, so that one may say, here is more, here is less of the Church? Does the meaning of the church hinge upon the loving fellowship of persons, or upon the ministry and ecclesiastical structure, or upon the way the gospel is proclaimed? At Lund was found, not a solution to these perennial problems, but a new approach to them. It is the way to Jesus Christ himself, as Lord and life of the Church. It was agreed that many of our deepest divergences in understanding the Church are due to disagreements as to the Person and saving work of Jesus Christ. Let us for a time leave the conventional issues of division and turn *together, in common* to consider afresh the meaning of our one Lord for his one Church.

The conference also took up some of the perplexing aspects of diverse ways of worship as these constitute barriers to unity. It is just in the realm of worship, said the report, "that disunity becomes explicit and the sense of separation most acute." At the same time, it is the testimony of the majority of delegates to ecumenical conferences that the surest sense of their unity in Christ comes during periods of common worship, however unfamiliar the liturgy may be, and even when an unknown language is used. Not only at conferences, but in their normal relations with congregations of other traditions in the same locality, Christians generally have the opportunity to experience both the estrangement and the attraction of diverse forms of worship. It is through these acts of adoration that the God who is adored effects the unity of his divided people.

Finally the Lund Conference sought to bring order into the confused discussion of the problem called Intercommunion. Is it not the most baffling situation imaginable that the Holy Communion, which is often called Christ's sacrament of unity, is precisely the act in which our divisions are most sharply discerned? The conference succeeded only in sorting out the various viewpoints with respect to this question and giving definition to the terms used to describe the several kinds of relationships which churches have established. It must be admitted that no more than slight progress was made toward a consensus on required conditions for participation in the Holy Communion.

The message of the conference was nevertheless a positive one, and there was less reluctance than in previous conferences to challenge the churches to act upon their frequent professions of love of unity. "Should not our Churches ask themselves whether they are showing sufficient eagerness to enter into conversation with other Churches," it asked; and further, "whether they should not act together in all matters except those in which deep differences of conviction compel them to act separately?" D. T. Niles observed sharply that the more usual case is for churches to do all things separately except those which *the world* demands that they do together! Such is not Christian obedience.

Not only the divisions of the Church but its slackness in mission was exposed at Lund to the light of God's purpose. In this light the interdependence of unity in mission and mission in unity was discerned. The I.M.C. had held in 1947 an important meeting in the little Canadian town of Whitby. In one of its prophetic declarations, this conference said: "Wherever devotion to local or denominational loyalties stands in the way of response to the larger call of Christ, it must be transcended."

Since 1948 there had been in effect a close relationship whereby the World Council of Churches was "in association with the International Missionary Council." This association has done very much to keep alive the questions of mission and evangelism in the W.C.C., and to encourage participants in the I.M.C. to face directly the consequences of church divisions for the Christian mission as a whole. Year by year this association has brought the two bodies closer to each other in ways too numerous to mention. But one significant sign of their converging purposes was visible in 1952. At Lund the men of the Faith and Order movement spoke increasingly of evangelism. At the conference of the I.M.C. in Willingen, Germany, those concerned primarily with mission were asking the member councils of the I.M.C. to give more attention to the urgency of Christian unity.

To bring to an end this survey of half a century's momentous development in the direction of church unity, we look briefly at the World Council's second Assembly, held in Evanston (U.S.A.) in 1954. It was first of all an important occasion for testing the vitality of the Council after its first six years. Some wondered whether there would be as much interest as at Amsterdam, when excitement ran high because of the newness and historical significance of the event. Such doubts were dispelled at Evanston, where the enthusiasm not only of American Christians but of visitors from all the world was greater than ever. And enthusiasm was matched by seriousness of purpose. In the study sections the delegates struggled together with the implications for faith and daily life of the theme, "Christ the Hope of the World." Then in six specific areas of study—faith and order, evangelism, racial and ethnic tensions, social questions, international relations, and the layman's vocation—they worked still further to know the mind of Christ. Special urgency attached to all these matters because of two factors of monumental importance: the amazingly rapid social and political revolution in Africa and Asia since 1945, and the grim contest between communism and free democracy in the world at large. This time there was not the slightest question about adequate representation from the churches of Asia and Africa. Their delegates were vocal, and were heeded. Never before had the non-Roman Christians of the world demonstrated such solidarity as then, despite the political forces pressing in to disrupt it. Remembering that Jesus' call to discipleship carries with it the obligation to die unto oneself, the delegates had little patience with smooth-worn platitudes as they wrote their reports. Nor was there the sound of hollowness in the words which the Assembly sent to the congregations of their more than 160 churches throughout the world: "Only at the Cross of Christ, where men know themselves as forgiven sinners, can they be made one. . . . And those who know that Christ is risen should have the courage to expect new power to break through every human barrier."

chapter **5**

Churches Becoming What They Are—One Church

WHEN THE APOSTLE PAUL wrote to the contentious Christians of Corinth, "You are the body of Christ," he was not flattering them with the implication that they were living up to their calling. They *were* the body of Christ, and yet must continually strive to *become* the body. So with the divided groups and blocs of Christians today. They *are* the one Church, but must still *become* the one Church. Unity in Christ has been given, it is now present, though hindered and obscured by divisions. As faithful and obedient Christians we are called to make that unity a visible, experienced way of living together as brothers in the love of Christ.

The long history of unitive movements in the Church, which we have been scanning, is becoming better known than it used to be. And most Christians have some idea of the existence and significance of the World Council of Churches. But the question they keep asking is: Do these movements really lead churches to unity? Are not the denominational barriers just as rigid and impassable as ever? There are many Christians—far too many—who are entirely indifferent to the scandal of divisions and have little interest in healing them. But there are also great numbers who are utterly impatient with the widespread devotion to separate denominations and factions in the Church. These people think that the theologians and church leaders are too cautious about seeking full union. They are impatient for the churches to get on with the job of reunion, that is, to become what they are. But there are two kinds of impatience; and Christian zealots who call for the immediate attainment of desirable ends do not always see the difference between them.

The first kind of impatience is irresponsible and unwise, however worthy its intentions. Let us bypass all these vexing questions of Faith and Order, it is often said. What if Anglicans are sticky on episcopacy and Baptists on believers' baptism? Unity is the important thing. Now, what shall we call the new church? The second kind is no less sincere. It recognizes that divisions are not superficial scratches in the skin but deep wounds in the flesh. There is a required length of time for healing the ancient quarrels and misunderstandings of the churches. Hastiness recommended in order to bring about the earliest possible union is likely to involve not only a disregard for the truth of the gospel but a careless and loveless unconcern for the weaker brother. Wounds badly healed leave ugly scars. Unions consummated before the right time and circumstance cause further ill-feeling and more divisions.

Having issued this warning, we must now take note of the little-known facts about church union in this present century. Already there have taken place so many unions of previously divided churches that only a few people can keep track of them all. Counting the complete mergers of churches, as well as close federation and official agreements on intercommunion, we find about fifty. And equally significant is the fact that at the present moment more than thirty-five official negotiations between churches are in progress. Some of these deserve scrutiny because they point the way to solutions of the various major questions on which many churches still remain divided.

Church Unions Completed since 1910

Forty times in forty-seven years there have taken place the solemn and joyous formalities, always within the context of worship, in which two or more churches have become one. On twenty-three of these occasions, the uniting bodies all belonged to the same confessional family. For the most part, these unions in the same families have not involved doctrinal differences of great importance. Nevertheless, divisions between the churches prior to union were sometimes as deep and wide as those existing between churches of separate communions. These were caused by points of contention which were not doctrinal, but political, economic, or psychological.

For example, separate Lutheran churches in America have generally remained distinct according to the customs and language of the European countries from which the members came as immigrants. Their children and grandchildren felt increasingly American and decreasingly German or Norwegian or Swedish. They have sought, and are still seeking, Lutheran unity in America.

When the Church of Scotland and the United Free Church of Scotland became one body in 1929, they brought to an end a number of bitter divisions which began in the eighteenth century. The central issue of division was relationship of the church to the state. Other separate traditions and practices had developed, of course, and were held tenaciously by the more conservative members. But these were not immutable. When the Church of Scotland in 1921 loosened its alliance with the government, the difficulty in effecting the union was greatly decreased.

With American Methodists there were two divisive factors. One was the power given to bishops. One body, called the Methodist Protestant Church, desired more freedom for laymen and so became separate in 1830. Then in 1845 the issue of Negro slavery rent the largest Methodist denomination in two. After the emancipation of slaves by Abraham Lincoln, the memories of warfare and the sharply differing attitudes toward Negroes in the North and the South kept the Methodists apart. Many years of conciliation were required before the union of the three Methodist branches took place in 1939. But the question of full integration of Negro and white members in the same churches has received its most promising impetus in 1956. Legislation by the Methodist General Conference then paved the way toward abolition of racial division.

At seventeen services of union since 1910 there have come into existence new bodies constituted of two or more churches belonging to different confessional or denominational families. These are inevitably more interesting, though not always more important, than the first kind. The denominations involved have been the Presbyterians, Methodists, Congregationalists, Baptists, Anglicans, Disciples of Christ, and United Brethren. Of these, the Presbyterians (or Reformed) have been the most active.

The first major union of this type to occur in this period was that of the United Church of Canada. In the vast and thinly populated regions of Canada there was simply no possibility of ministering according to denominational preference to pioneers who settled on the great plains. Elsewhere there were small villages which had more separate churches than they could support. This obvious difficulty lent urgency to the activities of those who believed that the Church, on strictly theological grounds, must in any case be one. The early nineteenth-century immigrants, who came almost entirely from Great Britain, brought with them a confusing array of small parties within three large traditions—the Presbyterian, Methodist, and Congregationalist. By the end of that century these nearly twenty separate bodies had been reduced by family reunions to only the three. In 1902 a union was proposed by the Methodists, and soon this was accepted in principle by the other two. But the path to union was not an easy one. First a plan had to be worked out which would provide a form of government satisfying the three bodies. This was done successfully. Then a common confession of faith was required. The negotiators eventually agreed on twenty basic articles of faith. Since the ministries of all three were mutually accepted, the only remaining problems were organizational. At this point certain Presbyterians began working diligently to frustrate the union. They were not satisfied with regard to the doctrinal integrity of the Methodists and Congregationalists, nor with the proposed common confession of faith. It is probably true to say that their sense of solidarity as Scots played its role, as did other sociological factors. Further, they challenged the legal right of the General Assembly of their church to bind each congregation to a union. These opponents of union represented one-third of the Presbyterian members and one-sixth of the congregations. It was a bitter decision which the majority took when it decided to purchase union with the other two bodies at the cost of schism within their own. But this they did, and the United Church of Canada came into existence in 1925. The other Presbyterians continue in separation to the present, but relationships between them and other churches become increasingly friendly.

In many such unions of churches there are members who prefer to remain apart, continuing their former divisions. Whatever the reason for their continuance, whether doctrinal, political, or personal, it is often brought to wide public notice because they initiate legal proceedings in order to retain church property which might otherwise be claimed by the new united church. This is a dismal situation, which Paul decried in Corinth (1 Cor. 6:6), and which shames the Church of Christ before non-Christians. Grievous experiences of this kind in the past are making the present planners of church union examine very carefully the matters of legal title and possession of church properties. More important, it is making them less willing to bring unions to a consummation so long as there are dissenting minorities which for reasons of faith and conscience (but not malice or avarice) wish to remain separate. There is a joke about a villager who was asked how many churches there were where he lived. "We had four," replied the man; "then there was a church union, and now we have five!" But the humor is soured by the fact that such things have actually happened.

Under very unusual circumstances a union of eight main denominations was brought about in Japan in 1941. This was the Kyodan, or Church of Christ in Japan, in its first form. The words "brought about" are used quite literally, for the initiative was taken by the Japanese government. Especially during the desperate years of war, the government did not want to be bothered by having to deal independently with so many little groups of Christians. No alternative to union was offered. Some entered the union gladly and hoped it would last. Some entered grudgingly with hopes of becoming independent again. Some, such as the majority of Anglicans, remained outside, and their church was legally dissolved. We cannot go deeply into the motives and thoughts of these harassed Christians. Most were willing to admit that the union was based on a very unsteady foundation, even though they tried to agree on a basic confession of faith. In 1945, after the war, the Church of the Nazarene withdrew without delay. The Lutherans separated rather reluctantly, but in the knowledge that they could not remain without such doctrinal agreements as were unlikely to be attained. The Anglicans returned to their own church, now restored. So the Kyodan continued with mainly Methodist, Congregational, and Presbyterian elements. The American mission boards continue to give it the support of personnel and money. And very recently the Kyodan has adopted a confession of faith which will undergird its union with a strong and agreed doctrinal position. It is not likely that any other church unions will take place under similar circumstances. But the example of the Kyodan has shown two things: how really necessary is serious agreement on matters of faith and order, and how well the church can make use of an adverse historical situation.

The Church of South India is certainly the best known of all the unions which have taken place. It deserves this distinction because it is the first and only union in history which involves both nonepiscopal churches and those which have maintained the unbroken historic succession of bishops since the early church. The Anglicans in India were by no means careless in their regard for keeping the episcopacy as a gift of God to the Church. The Methodists in South India derived from British missions and therefore, like British Methodists as distinguished from the American, had no bishops. The South India United Church (1908), as we saw, was itself a union of Presbyterians and Congregationalists. Neither these nor the Methodists had any interest in abandoning the values of their own traditions and becoming wholly conformed to Anglicanism. But they agreed with what their South Indian spokesman had said at Lausanne: "We must have one Church."

The initiative was taken at Tranquebar in 1919. In this same year in America, the Episcopal Church and the Congregationalists had reached a tentative agreement on a plan to have the latter's ministers receive, if they so desired, episcopal ordination. In England, at the same time, Anglicans and Free Churchmen were discussing the possibilities of a "constitutional episcopacy." The controversy over approaches to Anglican-Free Church unity in Kenya had caused a storm in 1913 which was still stirring up the minds of those who desired such unity. Could this forbiddingly deep gulf between episcopal and nonepiscopal churches be bridged? The 31 Indians, with one Englishman and one American, at Tranquebar thought that it could be. Led by Bishop Azariah, they wrote their *Manifesto,* which was partly the work of the great American evangelist Sherwood Eddy. Though a Congregationalist, he believed that the "episcopal element" was needed in a united church. This document stated first the need for unity. Then it anticipated the 1927 report of the Lausanne Conference by citing the necessity of congregational, presbyteral, and episcopal elements in the church. Finally it commended union on the basis of the familiar Lambeth Quadrilateral.

The respective churches soon gave their official approval to union negotiations, although the Methodists did not join in the talks until 1925. Other non-Roman churches in South India declined invitations to take part. Strong moral support was given indirectly by the Lambeth Conference of 1920, which in its significant "Appeal to All Christian People" stressed the urgency of seeking visible unity of the whole Church on earth.

From that time until 1947 the negotiating churchmen toiled diligently to work out the best possible scheme of union. They struggled with questions of doctrine even when there appeared to be surface agreement, lest a consensus in committee prove to be unsound. Yet no serious obstacles were found to match that of the ministry. An easy settlement would be for all the churches to recognize the ministries of the others as being valid and regular. For the Anglicans, of course, this begged the whole question. Another easy way would be for all non-Anglican ministers to be ordained by a bishop. But this was repugnant to those who believed themselves already to be ministers of the Church of God. Finally it was agreed that following the inauguration of union there would be bishops consecrated in the historic succession and appointed to newly formed dioceses. Ministers ordained in the nonepiscopal churches before the union would not be reordained, but simply accepted in the united church. After union, however, all ordinations would be by bishops together with presbyters. At the end of a trial period of thirty years, the whole question could be reviewed in the light of experience. This novel and daring plan was adopted. In Madras in September, 1947, the congregations of a million Christians were represented in the forming of the Church of South India.

A hundred years earlier than this, an Anglican bishop from England had asked, "Is it then a hope too unreasonable to be entertained that the power which will heal the divisions of the Church at home may come from her distant fields of mission work?" This power became dramatically real in 1947. The uniting churches in South India agreed that they would never sever their relations of communion with the related churches in England and America whence they had arisen. For the churches of the Anglican Communion, especially, this has been a great problem of theology and conscience. The Church of India, Pakistan, Burma, and Ceylon was the first among them to accord limited recognition to the Church of South India. A definite though similarly limited recognition was given by the Church of England in 1955. Other churches are now considering the question. One cannot predict with certainty that the adventurous step taken at Madras will cause divided churches elsewhere to follow. But the hopes of many were expressed by Bishop Palmer in 1933: "Some obscure persons in South India are willing to make the first attempt to end . . . division. They are like men asking leave to go over the top. They know that they may die in the attempt, and that their attempt will fail if they are not followed."

Church Unions at Present Being Negotiated

It is sometimes assumed, but falsely, that the Church of South India's scheme of union is a universally applicable and workable one. This is denied by the very architects of that scheme. In each country or region where divided Christians seek union of their churches they must work out their own plan. But two rules were learned by those in South India to be universally valid. First, no union can be achieved if we keep asking how much "our church" stands to *lose* by entering a union with others. We should ask instead how much we may *gain* in such a union. Second, there can never be union if negotiating parties try to settle every disagreement in doctrine, theology, polity, and ethics before the act of union. As separate churches we must recognize in each other enough of the truth of Christ's gospel so that we can take the decisive, irrevocable step of committing ourselves to one another in union. Then by common experience we can *grow together in unity.*

This principle is perhaps of moderate importance for proposed mergers of churches belonging already to the same confessional family. There are at present at least five movements of this kind. The Presbyterian Church in the U.S.A. and the United Presbyterian Church, both large bodies, have united in 1958. Also in America there are two important mergers under way, involving three Lutheran bodies in one and four in the other. The rigorous Missouri Synod is not however a party to these negotiations. Lutheran churches and missions are also seeking union in Canada, India, Japan, Australia, and South Africa, and have achieved it in New Guinea and Madagascar.

Of the projected unions between dissimilar churches today we can note fifteen which are promising. The one which has been consummated in 1957 is that between the Congregational–Christian Churches and the Evangelical and Reformed Church in the United States. After negotiations lasting for many years and a severe setback through court litigation among the Congregationalists, this union joins more than two million persons in one United Church of Christ. It is not unusual that such unlike churches should have sought merger. The former stems from seventeenth-century British Independency and early American Puritanism, with a distinctly congregational polity. The other represents the previously mingled Lutheran and Reformed elements of German Protestantism. Yet they have found many affinities with one another. History and statistics make it clear that such unions between dissimilar traditions occur more often than those between similar ones. This is a fact worth pondering.

The two most significant union efforts of the day, so far as interests of all Christians are concerned, are that in Ceylon and that in North India and Pakistan. These both differ from the scheme of South India in two major ways. First, they include Baptists. So they must work out an agreed plan to satisfy both the Baptists and those who practice infant baptism with sponsors. The fact that the Baptist bodies in each case are numerically small is irrelevant theologically; so long as they are participants, their teaching must be taken very seriously. Second, since Anglicans are among the uniting churches, episcopacy is to be preserved, but not in the South India manner with the long period of trial. Instead there will be initial unification of the episcopal and nonepiscopal ministries by acts of "mutual commissioning" for wider service in the united church. The North India plan is complicated by the further need for unifying the Anglican episcopate with the episcopate of the Methodist Church in Southern Asia (which is not claimed to be in the historic succession from the apostles). The North India plan is especially worth noting because its participants have such far-flung relations. It is related directly to the Church of England and indirectly to all churches of the Anglican Communion; to Methodists in England, America, Australia, and New Zealand; to Congregationalists and Baptists in England; and to Presbyterians in America. What effect would a successful union have upon all these bodies?

Already there have been similar efforts involving Anglicans and some of these other traditions in Canada, Iran, and Nigeria, and a recent initiative in Ghana. Furthermore, there are two-way conversations between the Anglicans and Methodists in both England and America, although their concern is more for intercommunion than for full organic union. At the same time, current official negotiations between the Church of England and the Church of Scotland (Presbyterian) are approaching the question of episcopacy in a deep and thorough way, looking toward intercommunion and eventually perhaps to union.

In both New Zealand and Australia there have been discussions for many years among the Methodists, Congregationalists, and Presbyterians. They have naturally been encouraged by the fortunes of the United Church of Canada. After some lagging during the war years, these negotiations are again gathering momentum. In New Zealand the Associated Churches of Christ (which are related to the Disciples of Christ) have joined in. In both countries the Anglicans are at present considering how to reply to invitations to join these movements toward union.

Elsewhere, one finds the Methodists and Waldensians exploring ways to unity in Italy, and also in Argentina together with the Disciples of Christ. In Jamaica it is the Presbyterians, Disciples, and Congregationalists who have this aim. In Java there is favorable chance of the union of Reformed and Mennonite bodies. And in Madagascar the Congregationalists of the London Missionary Society, the Evangelical Mission of Paris, and the Society of Friends find their desire for unity stronger than their will to remain separate.

The delegates to the World Council of Churches' Assembly in 1954 could take no decisions with respect to church union. That is the responsibility of the churches. But they expressed themselves nevertheless in words of insight and power as they considered their oneness in Jesus Christ and the historical divisions of churches. For some churches, they declared, "witnessing may require obedience unto death. They may have to be prepared to offer up some of their accustomed, inherited forms of life in uniting with other Churches without complete certainty as to all that will emerge from the step of faith. . . . But when Churches have been ready in this sense 'to die with Christ,' they have found that He who raised Jesus from the dead is faithful and powerful still." Without the faithfulness and power of God, who called and cares for his own people, no unions or mergers could succeed. But by God's help many churches now divided are becoming in fact what by the grace and calling of God they already are.

Chapter 6

We Face Twelve Vital Questions

THE UNITY OF THE CHURCH concerns every Christian without exception. Not all Christians, of course, are consciously troubled by divisions. But none is ever outside the range of the fellowship of Christ's love. Therefore all are involved in the unity of the Church.

The average church member may feel quite detached from the matters we have discussed in this book. He can perhaps grasp the biblical revelation about the Church and see its reference to his own life in the local congregation. But these sweeping tides of history, the rise and fall of denominations, the world-wide movements for unity, may seem overwhelmingly large and therefore unreal to him. Large they are, but not unreal. Ultimately the effect of these movements is felt by every Christian, even as great national and international events finally touch the lives of humble citizens.

It is not the reality of Christian unity, but the awareness of it, which the Christian may easily miss. In some countries the lack of unity is less apparent than in others.

In Norway, Sweden, and Finland, for example, more than 90 per cent of the people are members of the national churches, which are Lutheran. The scandal of division is felt less keenly there than in South Africa or India, where many denominations exist side by side. Yet even where there are few divisions to be seen, the Christian should understand that the *wholeness* of God's Church is not being experienced in his large national church. The divisions in other countries are divisions in the one Church of God to which he belongs. The well-being of the whole Church on earth is the concern of each Christian. This wholeness, or catholicity, of the Church includes its unity. It is a distinct unity in Jesus Christ, and it embraces the personal relations between two or three brethren in Christ as well as the common tasks of the great ecclesiastical bodies of the world.

Having pondered the biblical teaching about the unity of the Church and looked quickly at the efforts of Christians to manifest it during many centuries, we remain confronted by twelve major questions. Perhaps no one can deal adequately with the implications of all of them. But men of special training and experience in theology have no monopoly on them. Every sincere Christian should give thought to each question.

1. What are the specific ways by which I, the individual Christian, can promote unity? In my own congregation, what can I do to smooth the discord between opposing factions? How can I help eliminate prejudices and extend the right understanding with regard to churches other than my own? How can I help make the Christians in my village or town become a living, serving,

worshiping, and witnessing community, held together in unity by the love of Jesus Christ?

2. How can we make sure that any movements toward closer unity of churches will not take that wrong course which leads to the suppression of diversity and freedom? The same Jesus Christ who unites us also gives us true freedom. It is human arrogance, not Christ's love, that brings about a visible unity which stifles personal freedom. Knowing the churches in our own land, can we see how they can be united without being uniform in doctrine and customs? How can their diversities be maintained in a united church without violating the essential truth of the gospel?

3. What do we learn from the Bible about the unity of the Church that makes us intolerant of every division which disrupts that unity? The Bible clearly teaches that the Church is meant to be one, and that its chief task is to preach the gospel to all persons in the world. If we believe the Bible to be the Word of God, have we any right to be tolerant of the divisions which break up the oneness of the Church and make it harder for it to fulfill its task? Concern for the unity of the Church, as we have seen, is not something we can have or not have according to our tastes. It is something which God himself lays upon us, upon every single one of us, as a duty to him. To be fully obedient to this duty, then, we need to study the Bible persistently and intelligently and learn what it has to teach us about the meaning of Christ and his Church.

4. On what basis can we decide, if necessary, between loyalty to a brother in Christ in our own neighborhood but of a different denomination, and loyalty to the members, traditions, and teachings of our own denomination

in other parts of the world? Specifically, should a Methodist consider it his first duty to join up with a Lutheran in his own village, or rather to strengthen his oneness with Methodists in other countries? Should a Presbyterian church give priority to church union in a particular region or to its relations with all other Presbyterian churches? Nearly all of the denominations or confessions now have their world-wide councils, alliances, or federations. Does our participation in the work of these bodies strengthen the whole Ecumenical Movement, or weaken it? Just where should our first loyalty be placed?

5. What is the difference between practical co-operation of the churches, both locally and nationally, and the organic union of churches? Does co-operation lead naturally to union? Is there a danger that Christians may confuse interchurch co-operation with true unity and therewith be content? Are the various councils of churches going to freeze the unity movement at the point of common projects in study and service? The future of the World Council of Churches, for example, hangs upon such questions. They are no less important for national and local councils.

6. Can we be sure of the real meaning of church membership? Who is a true member and who is not? Some churches want to include a whole society of persons, most of whom were baptized as infants. Other churches declare that only those Christians who have professed their faith prior to baptism may be regarded as members. Still others ask whether baptism is the sufficient manner of entering the church. What about confirmation? Is it the necessary completion of baptism? Does confirmation alone give the Christian the privilege of receiving the Holy Communion? All these are difficult and divisive questions. Christians

have strong convictions about them. Yet they have to be resolved before certain churches can unite with others.

7. Is there a way to reconcile the episcopal ministries with the nonepiscopal? We must not exaggerate the importance of this question, as some people do. The Church is much more than its ministry. And episcopal churches have as strong a concern for true doctrine and faithful evangelism as for the succession of bishops. On the other hand, we err if we just disregard this question or shrug it off as a peculiar interest of a few churches. Church union talks which involve Anglicans have shown that the question is unavoidable. A few solutions have been applied. The Church of South India has its trial period of thirty years, during which time the episcopal and nonepiscopal ministries exist within the same church. The union plans for North India and Ceylon call for the unification of diverse ministries at the outset. Which way is better?

8. How can we understand more clearly the way in which church unity is hindered by social, political, and cultural factors? Even if the questions of baptism, ministry, and biblical authority were agreed on by two divided churches, would not other nondoctrinal questions keep them apart? The love of power, language barriers, social and economic class distinctions, resistance to change of customs, and unbending loyalty to denominational traditions and institutions—these and many more must be understood by us. Then only may we act upon that understanding, and judge them in the light of the gospel as illegitimate reasons for continued division.

At the same time we need to recognize the way certain nondoctrinal influences hasten the movement toward unity. This side of the question is easily overlooked. For example, the effective use of material resources as an incentive for the unity of the churches is simply good stewardship of God's gifts. And the common experiences of Christians in war prison camps, in times of natural catastrophe, and under totalitarian persecution have shown the frailty of many of the causes for division which are normally defended with passion. The call of God to Christians, directing them to unite, comes not only from the Bible or through ecumenical conferences. It comes also from the clash and clatter of human society, the tension and turmoil of political events, wherein Christians find the need for showing that they all belong to one another in the one household of God.

9. Is the power of Christian love strong enough to defeat the divisive powers of racial conflict? The way human beings mistreat one another because of racial differences is a vicious evil. It is utterly contrary to God's will revealed in Jesus Christ. Thus it is contrary to the nature of the Church. Yet this kind of division penetrates the churches and sets Christian against Christian for the sole reason that the Christians' God made people to be different. What are the specific steps Christians in each country can take to attack and defeat this evil? Can the churches not be the place where true brotherhood is practiced and demonstrated?

10. What is the mutual responsibility of churches within the Ecumenical Movement and churches outside it with respect to the Lord's will for the unity of the whole Church on earth? There are great and spiritually healthy church bodies which are not members of the various church councils and have no wish to become members. Among these are the Roman Catholic Church, the Southern Baptist Convention, the Lutheran Church–Missouri

Synod, the Russian Orthodox Church, the Pentecostal and Holiness Churches, and many more. Some are indifferent to ecumenical work, some openly hostile to it. Some define church unity in terms of accepting their own doctrines only. Others hold that unity is a "spiritual" matter which requires no visible form. Membership in councils of churches is certainly no final test of a church's faith and love. But such membership should not be a cause for deepening divisions. Who has the truth of Christ? Can truth and unity be set in opposition to one another? Can truth and unity be known without love?

11. How can we foresee and avoid the dangers of a zealous but unwise "unionism"? Some people seem to believe that church unity is mainly an organizational question. Keep merging the denominations and eventually we shall have the one true Church! This idea ignores both the need for renewed faith and witness in the church, as well as the peril of the excessive concentration of power in church government. Most responsible church leaders decisively reject the notion that there should be one, centrally administered church organization of the world. Is it any less objectionable to establish too much centralized authority in countries or regions where there are millions of Christians? Is there a desirable limit to the administrative unit of a united church? Is there an optimum size of a united church, beyond which there is opportunity for bureaucracy and misused power to suppress Christian freedom?

12. What can we through our praying contribute to the manifesting of the unity of the Church? If the oneness of the Church is such an urgent need, and if it is constantly threatened and hindered by all kinds of divisions, we are without excuse as Christians if we do not implore God

regularly to unite his people and heal their schisms. Prayer for unity should be our daily prayer. It should be as normal as our prayer for daily bread and the coming of God's kingdom. The thought which should make us conscious of this need arises from Jesus' own prayer. If at the time of his passion and death our Lord was moved to pray "that they may be one," ought not we his followers to continue that prayer, until by God's power and wisdom and love it shall be answered in his own way?

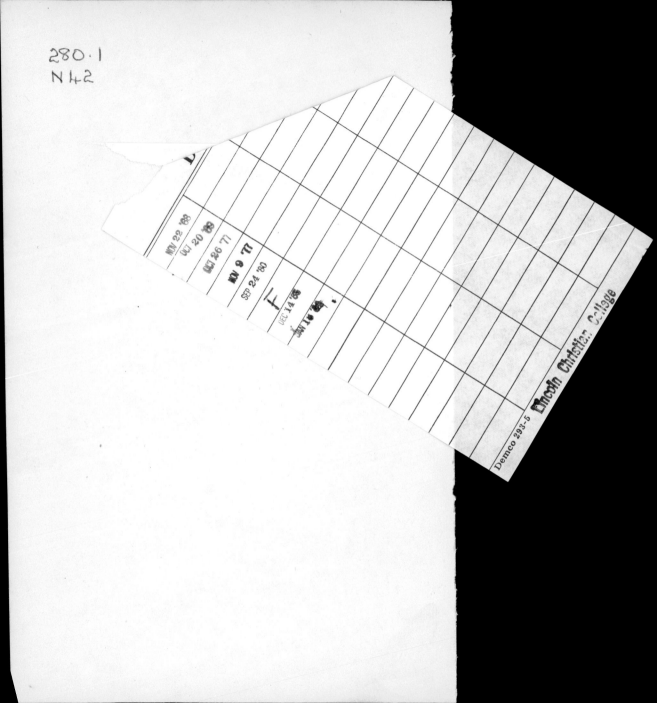